Presented to

_____

by

_____

on

_____

TIME OUT!
A Men's Devotional

Compiled by
Clint and Mary Beckwith

Evergreen Communications, Inc.
Ventura, California

TIME OUT!
A MEN'S DEVOTIONAL

Published by:
Evergreen Communications, Inc.
2085 Sperry Avenue
Ventura, CA 93003

Scripture quotations in this publication are taken from the following:

KJV — King James Version.
MLB — Scripture taken from the MODERN LANGUAGE BIBLE: THE BERKELEY VERSION IN MODERN ENGLISH. Copyright © 1945, 1959, 1969 by Zondervan Publishing House. Used by permission.
NASB — Scripture taken from the New American Standard Bible, © 1960, 1962, 1963, 1968, 1971, 1972, 1973, 1975, 1977 by The Lockman Foundation. Used by permission.
NIV — From the Holy Bible, New International Version. Copyright © 1973, 1978, 1984 International Bible Society. Used by permission of Zondervan Bible Publishers.
NKJV — From the New King James Version. Copyright © 1979, 1980, 1982, Thomas Nelson Inc., Publishers. Used by permission.
RSV — From Revised Standard Version of the Bible, copyrighted 1946 and 1952 by the Division of Christian Education of the NCCC, U.S.A.
TLB — Scripture verses are taken from The Living Bible © 1971 owned by assignment by Illinois Regional Bank N.A. (as trustee). Used by permission of Tyndale House Publishers, Inc., Wheaton, IL 60189. All rights reserved.

Library of Congress Cataloging-in-Publication Data

Beckwith, Clint, 1942-
    Time out! a men's devotional.

    1. Men — Prayer-books and devotions — English. II. Beckwith, Mary, 1945- .
BV4843.T56 1989 242'.642 — dc20   89-37908
ISBN 0-926284-00-2

95 94 93 92 91 90 89   9 8 7 6 5 4 3 2 1

Printed in the United States of America

*Dedicated to
the joys of our lives:
Rob, Alan, Laura, and Russ*

CONTENTS

PREFACE

Time Out! is a collection of over one hundred brief — and practical — devotions, written by men for men, all designed to give you the reader a few minutes of relaxation and refreshment, time out from your busy schedule.

From husbands and fathers to singles and sons, from pastors and professionals to laymen and students, forty authors share personal experiences and thoughts on Christian living.

Each devotion begins with a passage from the Bible and ends with a short prayer, and there's plenty of space throughout the book to jot down special thoughts and inspirations of your own.

The Apostle Paul said in his letter to the Philippians, "Whatever it takes, I will be one who lives in the fresh newness of life" (3:11, *TLB*). We believe you'll experience fresh newness as you enjoy the devotions written just for you in our men's devotional, *Time Out!*

The Right Man for the Job

Donald L. Evans, Jr.

*For thou didst form my inward parts, thou didst
knit me together in my mother's womb.*
Psalm 139:13, *RSV*

I watched with interest as construction began on the condominium complex in the field behind my house. The first task was the removal of some trees from the one-time orchard and the demolition of an old, abandoned, two-story farmhouse.

I looked on in fascination while the operator deftly maneuvered the huge earth mover. His skill was such that he could uproot a large tree, carry it off, and then break it into pieces the size of his choosing.

With the same powerful machine, he did delicate work as well. I was amazed as he picked up a one-and-a-half inch piece of pipe used as a marker stake, and then relocated it ten feet from the original spot. That task would be like trying to pick up a toothpick with a posthole digger.

When the man stopped the juggernaut for a break, I expressed my admiration.

"Man! You can really make that thing dance!"

He smiled at me and said, "Well, I've been operating this machine for many years."

It struck me that if I tried to drive that big 'dozer, I would make a mess of whatever I tried to accomplish. I know nothing about its capabilities, nor how it works. The man I watched knew everything about that machine. He was obviously the best man to have at the controls.

I thought about the times I had tried to run my life without God's guidance and ended up making a mess of things. God made me, and He knows everything there is to know about me, past, present, and future. The next time I want to run things in my life on my own, I'll remember the bulldozer operator, and I'll put the One in control who can do the job right.

Father, forgive me when I try to run things on my own without you. I affirm your wisdom and lordship in my life. Amen.

Choose Joy!

W. Terry Whalin

But godliness with contentment is great gain.
1Timothy 6:6, *NIV*

Sweat dripped down my nose and onto the front of my shirt. I tried to relax and keep up with Francis, my running partner.

Each day at lunchtime we pound the pavement and get a glimpse of the ocean located only two miles from our office. The clear blue sky meant heavy beach traffic as people flocked to the Pacific's sand and surf.

The miles slipped past as Francis and I moved slowly enough for exercise and good conversation. Suddenly a truck with two teens passed us and water slapped against my shirt and face. Despite my five years of running, water thrown from a passerby was a unique experience. At that instant, I lost all sense of self-control and began to shout and shake my fist at the truck, but the driver never heard my retort. Dripping wet, I lacked two miles to reach the office. Then the scene struck me as funny — and refreshing. We laughed and continued our run.

Today the unexpected may catch me again by surprise. Do I lose control, shout, and then get depressed, or simply laugh it off? If I shout with anger, it may ruin my day, but if I choose to be joyful, I can feel refreshed and strengthened.

Lord, help me to see the unexpected with a light heart, and choose joy. Amen.

Hurricane!

Brad Sargent

*We are no longer to be children, tossed here and
there by waves, and carried about by every wind of
doctrine, by the trickery of men, by craftiness in
deceitful scheming.* Ephesians 4:14, *NASB*

If I'd known what I was about to go through, I
would've stayed on the docks at Oslo. But I boarded the
Braemar, an eight-deck ferry that would sail me from
Norway to England. The next day found us smack dab in
the middle of a North Sea hurricane!

The storm recorded winds of ninety miles per hour,
fifteen more than the minimum level to be designated a
hurricane. That abstract number became absolutely
concrete to me during the forty-three-hour trip.

The huge *Braemar* rocked back and forth nine times
each minute for endless hours. I felt like the metal ball
that's bounced from post to post in a pinball machine.
Other passengers must've felt similarly. Nearly all the sea-

sickness buckets, strategically placed every two or three paces along every hallway, were gone by trip's end.

The crew tried to maintain an appearance of calm and normalcy by keeping to their regular schedule. But that was impossible. Tables went topsy-turvy. Dishes fell and broke. Waiters dropped their trays. Everyone tripped trying to hold their balance and walk. They even canceled a movie because the projector crashed to the aisle.

The damage on land was even worse. The hurricane had knocked out phone and power lines. Fouling up transportation were uprooted trees across roads and train tracks. What a mess!

I stayed at a bed and breakfast. Fortunately, they had a good supply of candles plus two kerosene lamps. But no refrigerator. No heat in the rooms. Clothes, washed by hand and line dried. Simple meals, cooked on an oil-heated stove. As one frustrated native commented, "This is like going back a hundred years!"

Now I understand why the Apostle Paul used a "winds and waves" illustration to depict the effects of erroneous doctrine and deceits of man. These "storms" make you spiritually sick. You can't keep up the appearance that everything's okay because it caves in around you. You're off balance. Roadblocks confront you everywhere. Communication between you and God stops. The spiritual power in your life temporarily disconnects, and, eventually, you revert to the old ways you functioned before The Power Source came into your world.

Life will always contain breezes of false doctrine, because we are fallen beings living in a broken world. We can, however, prevent these winds from becoming hurricanes by heeding God's Word and learning from the gifted men He provides to His Body (Ephesians 4:1-13).

Thank you, Father, that Jesus is the Way, the Truth, and the Life. Help me learn of you and trust you to calm the storms of error in my life. Amen.

On the Road Again

Tony Sbrana

Be imitators of God, therefore, as dearly loved
children and live a life of love, just as Christ loved
us and gave himself up for us as a fragrant offering
and sacrifice to God. Ephesians 5:1-2, *NIV*

I hate driving. I do. Well, okay, not always.
Sometimes, if weather and traffic conditions are
unusually favorable, I can achieve a kind of obliviousness
to my chronic automotive angst. But stick me in the fast
lane behind some Sunday driver with a perpetually
blinking turn signal and something angry stirs inside.
Surround me on all sides with a legion of frustrated, five
o'clock freeway slaves and it's all over! I'm sorry to admit
it, but, if it's true that the thought is as bad as the deed, I'm
guilty of vehicular manslaughter a hundred times over.

And often I prayed that God would cause me to love
driving. He didn't. Instead He revealed a bit of truth to me.

He doesn't want me to love driving. He wants me drive loving. In other words, it's not my attitude *towards* driving that matters, it's my attitude *while* driving.

The fact that I'm in a hurry doesn't make the sightseer in front of me the enemy. *Drive loving.* The fact that I have to brake suddenly because someone cuts me off doesn't justify downshifting into "attack mode." *Drive loving.*

Of course, the issue isn't just driving. There are lots of things that I dislike: helping with the dishes, folding the laundry, dealing with the boss, paying the bills, figuring out the taxes.

And even when the tasks and expectations are a lot more serious — requiring real courage, endurance, or sacrifice — the truth remains the same. The ultimate example was set for us nearly two thousand years ago. His anguished prayer in Gethsemane and His words of grace at Calvary make it perfectly clear. Christ didn't love dying. But He most definitely died loving.

Dear Lord, often I don't feel very loving. Grant me the grace to act lovingly anyway, and to daily yield my heart to the transforming power of your Holy Spirit, our infinite and accessible source of love. Amen.

A Promise to Pray

James C. Dobson

The effectual fervent prayer of a righteous man availeth much. James 5:16, *KJV*

I'll never forget the time a few years ago when our daughter had just learned to drive. Danae had been enrolled in Kamakazi Driving School and the moment finally arrived for her to take her first solo flight in the family car. Believe me, my anxiety level was climbing off the chart that day. Someday you will know how terrifying it is to hand the car keys to a sixteen-year-old kid who doesn't know what she doesn't know about driving.

Shirley [my wife] and I stood quaking in the front yard as Danae drove out of sight. We then turned to go back into the house and I said, "Well, Babe, the Lord giveth and the Lord taketh away." Fortunately, Danae made it home safely in a few minutes and brought the car to a careful and controlled stop. That is the sweetest sound in the world to an anxious parent!

It was during this era that Shirley and I covenanted between us to pray for our son and daughter at the close of every day. Not only were we concerned about the risk of an automobile accident, but we were also aware of so many other dangers that lurk out there in a city like Los Angeles. Our part of the world is known for its weirdos, kooks, nuts, ding-a-lings, and fruitcakes. That's one reason we found ourselves on our knees each evening, asking for divine protection for the teenagers whom we love so much.

One night we were particularly tired and collapsed into bed without our benedictory prayer. We were almost asleep before Shirley's voice pierced the night. "Jim," she said, "we haven't prayed for our kids yet today. Don't you think we should talk to the Lord?"

I admit it was very difficult for me to pull my 6'2" frame out of the warm bed that night. Nevertheless, we got on our knees and offered a prayer for our children's safety, placing them in the hands of the Father once more.

Later we learned that Danae and a girl friend had gone to a fast-food establishment and bought hamburgers and cokes. They drove up the road a few miles and were sitting in the car eating the meal when a city policeman drove by, shining his spotlight in all directions. He was obviously looking for someone, but gradually went past.

In a few minutes, Danae and her friend heard a "clunk" from under the car. They looked at one another nervously and felt another sharp bump. Before they could leave, a man crawled out from under the car and emerged on the passenger side. He was very hairy and looked like he had been on the street for weeks....The man immediately came over to the door and attempted to open it. Thank God, it was locked. Danae quickly started the car and drove off...no doubt at record speed.

Later, when we checked the timing of this incident, we realized that Shirley and I had been on our knees at the precise moment of danger. Our prayers were answered. Our daughter and her friend were safe!

Lord, thank you for the privilege and power of prayer. Never let us forget that you have given us a major role in the lives of our children, not only to love them and provide for their daily needs, but to be their prayer warriors as well. Amen.

Adapted from the book *Love For A Lifetime* by Dr. James C. Dobson, copyright 1987 by James C. Dobson. Published by Multnomah Press, Portland, Oregon 97266. Used by permission.

The Performance Trap

John R. Strubhar

I can do all things through Him [Christ] who strengthens me. Philippians 4:13, *NASB*

I'm just like you. Without realizing it, I get caught in the performance trap! Wherever I turn, someone is talking about performing.

Management executives design elaborate performance programs for their personnel. Agriculturists are concerned about the performance yield of their crops. Olympic athletes discipline their bodies in order to perform great feats of strength and stamina. One of America's leading oil companies, Phillips Petroleum, bills itself as the "performance company."

Even in the Church, there is great pressure upon pastors, and laity alike, to perform, to live up to the expectations placed upon them by their peers and fellow believers. Oftentimes, such demands lead to frustration

31

and resentment because of well-meaning but unrealized or unfulfilled expectations.

Here is a bit of wisdom that has helped me: *You can never accomplish everything that others expect of you; you can never accomplish everything that you expect of yourself; but you can always accomplish everything that God expects of you.*

The Apostle Paul wrote to the Philippians, "For I am confident of this very thing, that He who began a good work in you will perfect (perform) it until the day of Christ Jesus" (1:6, *NASB*). What God begins to perform in our lives, He always perfects! There is no "performance lag" with Him. Indeed, He always finishes that which He initiates.

Dr. F. B. Meyer, the great Bible teacher, has written, "We go to the artists' studios and find their unfinished pictures covering large canvasses, and suggesting great designs, but which have been left, either because the genius was not competent to complete the work, or because paralysis laid the hand low in death; but, as we go into God's great workshop, we find nothing that bears the mark of haste or insufficiency of power to finish."

There will always be those expectations that supercede our human abilities, but the bottom line is that our work is God's work! Through the resurrection power of Jesus Christ, we can perform that *which He expects of us.* What a relief that is!

Lord, help me today to meet your performance standards. My ultimate desire is to please you and accomplish your agenda for my life. Amen.

Rivers of
Living Water

Herman D. Rosenberger

*He who believes in me, as the Scripture has said, out
of his heart will flow rivers of living water.*
John 7:37, *NKJV*

Many years ago I traveled down the Mississippi
River from St. Paul, Minnesota, to the Gulf of Mexico, a
distance of two thousand miles. The ship I traveled on
was a newly launched, 320-foot, 4,000 ton U.S. Navy
vessel. I was a member of the skeleton crew designated to
bring the ship to New Orleans, Louisiana, where it was to
be commissioned.

During the two weeks required to make the trip, I
became well acquainted with the Mississippi River. I
learned that the character and physical appearance of the
river properly divided into three stages. From Lake Itasca,
its source, to the head of navigation at St. Paul, it is a clear
fresh stream winding through low countryside dotted

with lakes and marshes. From St. Paul to the mouth of the Missouri River, it flows into a powerful, dominating river. Flowing past steep limestone bluffs, it gathers in many rivers and streams from Minnesota, Wisconsin, Illinois, and Iowa. The character of the river at this point caused the Algonkian-speaking Indians to name the river "The Father of Waters." At Cairo, Illinois, the Ohio River junctions with the Mississippi at which time it reaches its full grandeur.

As I reflect on that extraordinary trip down the Mississippi, I am reminded of Jesus' promise to the believer: "Out of his heart will flow rivers of living water." Of course, Jesus was referring to the indwelling of the Holy Spirit (John 7:39). The function of the Mississippi is somewhat analogous to the function of the Spirit in the believer's life. The Mississippi provides water, navigation, fishing, generation of electicity, and recreation. In the spiritual sense, the Holy Spirit quenches the thirst of the soul, provides navigation for life, generates power for witness, and gives rest and re-creation for the soul.

Lord, fill me with your Holy Spirit today so that out of my heart the rivers of living water may flow. Amen.

Busy for God

Grayson F. Wyly

Present your bodies a living sacrifice, holy,
acceptable unto God, which is your reasonable
service. Romans 12:1, *KJV*

Most of my youth was spent living on the New Jersey seashore, where my friends and I found many things to occupy our time: swimming, riding the waves, beach parties, miniature golf, and going to Asbury Park to hear the sounds of the big bands. Yet, even with all those attractions, I can remember times when we didn't know what to do with ourselves.

However, after the Lord Jesus Christ became Lord of my life, I became busy for God — my life became full. I had choir practice, Bible studies, prayer meetings, young people's meetings, and I was on summer staff at Word of Life Island. Even the mundane things of life were for the Lord.

Then came marriage and children, deacons' meetings, treasurer's reports, and leading Bible studies. My life was still busy, but I was using different talents and abilities.

Now I'm retired, and although life is still abundantly full, I wonder how I was able to keep up with everything while I was working a full-time job. In my Bible beside Romans 12:3, I penciled a note that reads, "God accepts my limitations." The inference is *and so must I.*

Now that I'm slowing down somewhat I have to remember that my estimation of myself must be sober, not lofty, while accepting the talents I now possess to be used for the Lord. We all have limitations, but still plenty of abilities, talents and gifts to keep busy for God.

Father, please keep my attitudes about my abilities and talents sober. And help me to rightly evaluate the gifts you have graciously given to be used for your glory, so that I may present them as a reasonable service to you. Amen.

Reflections from a Church Nursery

Michael B. Reynolds

*And we know that in all things God works for the
good of those who love Him, who have been called
according to His purpose.* Romans 8:28, *NIV*

Jerry takes the ball from Robbie and gives him a hard
shove. Robbie falls backward, landing on his well-
diapered rump. There is a pause, then the crying begins. I
know the issue is not the physical pain but simple
injustice. Robbie had the ball first, but Jerry, age two,
aggressively took it, adding the knockdown to make it
final.

I put one arm around Robbie and with the other arm
grab another ball. It's not the same size or color, but
Robbie doesn't seem to mind. He is up on his feet again,
and off to play with the stand-in ball.

Why is it that I, as an adult, do not insist on justice?
Jerry was unfair and took what someone else had first

rights to. I could retrieve the ball from Jerry and restore it to Robbie, and even give Jerry a talking to or a simple form of punishment, like sitting in a chair.

However, my age and experience give me a perspective these kids don't have. I know how unimportant balls are. I also know the attention span of these kids. I substitute a second ball for the first, because I know in thirty seconds both boys will be pursuing other things.

Perhaps I have a duty to correct Jerry, although the overall welfare of the nursery this evening may hinge on keeping Jerry content. If I confront him with his aggressiveness, he will not understand. And if he senses too much rejection from me, he might go into one of his crying rampages. His shrill cry will quickly stir the other children and turn the calm nursery into pandemonium.

Could it be that God uses this sort of reasoning in dealing with us? Sometimes our humanness clouds our perspective, and like children, we fail to realize just how unimportant some things really are. When we long for a change of circumstances, perhaps a better car, a nicer home, or a bigger salary, God knowingly keeps a proper perspective. As in Robbie's attachment to the ball, God's decision about us may reflect His knowledge that within thirty hours or thirty days this particular need or desire will no longer exist.

God's activity in our lives is normally based on more information than we have access to. He has a bigger picture of the circumstances, one that sees the future as well as the past and one that sees every other person and his personal needs as well.

Working in the nursery has helped me better understand Romans 8:28. I can't protect every child all the time. They may stumble over toys, spill their little cups of water, or have conflicts with one another. However, I do strive for their well-being with all of the grace and love I can muster.

And so does God with us!

Lord, there are injustices happening all around me. Help me to understand that even what seems unfair has a place in your perfect plan. Amen.

Knowing the Best from the Good

Harold J. Sala

This is the way; walk in it. Isaiah 30:21, *NIV*

W hen you hear someone say of a male friend, "He's really a success!" what do you understand that to mean? Is the "successful" person making a lot of money, is his career going well, is he rapidly climbing the greasy ladder of corporate success?

Could those words ever mean that a man is a terrific dad, great lover, faithful husband, and provider of his wife's needs?

An area of great concern for many women today is the relationship of men to their families. Torn by the pressures of carving out a successful career and being a good husband and father, a lot of men find they come up short of success in both areas. Feeling the barb of criticism and the frustration of failure, some men retreat and walk out.

What *do* wives want from their husbands? Perhaps in

the family room, they would like companionship; in the kitchen, some support; in the bedroom, tenderness and intimacy. But is all of this too much for a man to deliver?

As males, our relationships have become fragmented by time, strained by weariness, and structured by the constant demands made upon us to perform. We have lost tenderness, compassion, sensitivity, intimacy, and feelings. Many of us have, however, succeeded in filling our homes with a multitude of gadgets soon to need repair or replacement, but we have obtained them at tremendous cost.

Men, maybe it's time for us to reject the promotion that gives us a bit more money but demands even more of our time, to learn again that the important things in life — the love of a wife, the smile of a child, the beauty of our work — cannot be bought at any price. It's late, but it's not too late for us to rediscover our true masculinity.

Father, I'm torn in so many different directions that it's tough to keep my priorities straight. Help me to reject the loudest voice for the most important one and to know the best from the good. And help me start today. Amen.

Angel in a Dismal Place

Larry E. Clark

Moses...was not aware that his face was radiant.
Exodus 34:29 *NIV*

The man in the overcoat stood on a street corner in a dismal section of the city, one of the rabble that gathered. At first I didn't notice him. I was with a group of young people, our night to visit skid row and sing and tell the good news of Christ. Derelicts surrounded us as we stood on the street corner. Some mocked, others stared out of bleary eyes.

Gradually the man arrested my attention. A faded and worn overcoat covered him from head to knee, a scarf slung around his neck warded off the cold of the evening, while a stocking cap held down a mat of unruly, grizzled hair.

But his eyes! They blazed with joy. His whole face was alight with a radiance that kept me aware of him.

Only with difficulty could I keep my eyes off of him.

Various ones of us told of our faith in the Lord. As we challenged the men to trust in our Lord, the man in the overcoat suddenly opened his mouth and declared, "Marvelous Christ!" Those words he repeated over and over, not flippantly but enunciating them with conviction, out of a full heart.

I've never seen that man since. But I've often wondered who he was. An angel in disguise? Maybe. But he stood among his fellow derelicts as a simple but powerful testimony to the grace of God.

Lord, help me to radiate your love even in dismal places. Amen.

Purity Won a Hearing

Charles R. Swindoll

But examine everything carefully; hold fast to that
which is good; abstain from every form of evil.
1 Thessalonians 5:21-22 *NASB*

When I was in the Marines, I spent nearly a year
and a half in the Orient. Some of the time I was stationed
in Japan, most of the time on the island of Okinawa. Eight
thousand lonely miles away from my wife and family. Lots
of free time...and plenty of opportunities to drift into
sexual escapades. Most of the men in my outfit regularly
shacked up in the village. For those who didn't want the
hassle of a "commitment" to one woman, there was an
island full of available one-nighters. Brightly lit bars, with
absolutely gorgeous (externally, that is) females of any
nationality you pleased, were open seven nights a week,

365 days a year. And there wasn't anything they wouldn't do to satisfy their customers who were mostly Marines. The sensual temptation was fierce, to say the least.

I was in my mid-twenties. I was Christian. I was also one-hundred-percent human. It didn't take me long to realize that unless I learned how to force my body to behave, I'd be no different from any other Marine on liberty. Without getting into all the details, I developed ways to stay busy. I occupied my time with creative involvements. When walking along the streets, I walked fast. I refused to linger and allow my body to respond to the glaring come-on signals. My eyes looked straight ahead...and sometimes I literally *ran* to my destination. I consciously forced myself to tune out the sensual music. I disciplined my mind through intensive reading, plus a Scripture memory program. And I began most days praying for God's strength to get me through. The battle was terribly difficult, but the commitment to sexual purity paid rich dividends, believe me.

It worked, and it will work for you too. Now, before you think I'm the monk type, let me declare to you *nothing could be further from the truth.* I simply refused to let my body dictate my convictions. Just as 1 Thessalonians 4:3-7 implies, moral purity paid off. And by the way, when the Lord began to open doors for me to talk about Christ with others, it is remarkable how willing they were to listen. Down deep inside, behind all that macho mask, the men longed to be rid of that awful, nagging guilt...the other side of sexual impurity that the merchants of hedonism never bother to mention. Purity won a hearing.

Dear heavenly Father, give me strength each day to shun

*evil. Give me wisdom to examine all things carefully. Help
me to hold fast to that which is good in order that I might
bring glory to you. Amen.*

Old Duke

Leonard W. DeWitt

I will fear no evil: for thou art with me.
Psalm 23:4, *KJV*

What I'm about to share is more than a boy's love for an old horse. It's really an account of God's protection.

I grew up on a farm in the province of Alberta, in Western Canada. Until I was twelve years old, we used horses to do most of our farm work. "Old Duke" was the name we affectionately tagged to the horse our family used to pull our buggy. Until we bought our first car, an old Model-T Ford, the buggy was our primary means of transportation, except for winter, when we used an enclosed sleigh.

One summer Sunday, Old Duke was taking my family (except my dad) home from Sunday School and church. We were about one mile out of town when Old Duke suddenly stopped. No amount of coaxing by my mother could persuade that horse to take one more step forward. In fact, he began to back up and, with unbelievable skill,

47

he maneuvered the buggy and our family off the road and down into the ditch. It's hard to imagine that a big-rig driver could have done any better.

Moments later our attention was drawn to a loud roar and a cloud of dust coming from the direction we had just traveled. Suddenly, two cars racing side by side on that narrow dirt road thundered by. If we had still been on the road, in all likelihood, we would have been seriously injured or killed. One of the drivers stopped, came back, and checked to see if we were okay. By then Old Duke had skillfully pulled us back up on the road, ready to take us on home.

My mother assured the man we were okay, but no thanks to him. He asked our forgiveness and told how he had witnessed our wonder horse deftly removing us from the path of danger. He said, "Someone was surely watching over you."

How did Old Duke know of the danger speeding our way from behind us? How did he know what to do?

Throughout my life I have again and again witnessed God as my protector. The Psalmist says that the Lord is our "shield and buckler, our high tower and sure defense" (Psalm 119:114).

Old Duke will always be a cherished memory. More importantly, I marvel and rejoice in God's present watchful care and protection. The Twenty-third Psalm sums it up correctly: "I will fear no evil: for thou art with me."

Thank you, Father, for watching over me. Thank you for being my protector and my sure defense. Amen.

A Lesson on Listening

Charles R. Brown

Pay attention to what I say; listen closely to my
words. Do not let them out of your sight.
Proverbs 4:20-21, *NIV*

Our number two son joined me one afternoon in
my office at home. Five-year-old Mike brought some toys
to play with while I worked. He parked cars and trucks on
a nearby stuffed chair and we talked. Well, mostly, he
talked. I was enjoying the simple pleasure of being with
him.

As I busied myself at the desk, Mike said, "Daddy."

"A-huh," I replied.

"Daddy."

"I'm listening, son, while I'm working here."

"No, Daddy," he persisted. "Listen to me with your
face!"

He wanted my undivided attention and with one little line he grabbed it with lightning speed.

I have often wondered how many opportunities I have missed for life-changing dialogue with my children, my wife, and my friends, who seek my attention only to receive second-hand listening.

How often I have settled for something less than the best, while preoccupied with the "busyness" of my life as God says to me, "Listen, for I have worthy things to say" (Proverbs 8:6).

Father, help me to truly listen to my children, my wife, my pastor, my friends. Most of all, help me to listen intently to what you have to say to me. Amen.

God Gives
Us Joy

Richard Cornelius

Rejoice in the Lord alway: and again I say, Rejoice.
Philippians 4:4, *KJV*

In the summer of 1988, I had an experience that
changed my life dramatically. The results of an angiogram
revealed I needed triple by-pass heart surgery. I was
fearful of surgery but knew I had no choice. Following the
operation there were intense moments during recovery.
But God granted me the grace to live through it.

Every day now I realize that life is a gift from God. I
am more aware each day of how much there is around
me to enjoy. Flowers are blooming everywhere; orange
trees are in full bloom, with a fragrance that only God
could create; a boy dances under a large sprinkler,
catching water in his mouth; the many birds in the park
busily go about their daily routine, looking for food. All of

these things bring new pleasures.

Psalm 118:24 gives a new ring to my heart: "This is the day which the Lord hath made; we will rejoice and be glad in it" *(KJV)*. Each day I thank God, praise Him, and rejoice that He has allowed me the privilege of living one more day. Regardless of my health or any other problem I may have, I am grateful to my heavenly Father for life. God is so good.

Dear Lord, thank you for each new day and for allowing me the real joy of knowing you. Help me to share your goodness with others. Amen.

Like Lost Sheep

Lloyd John Ogilvie

*And when he finds it, he joyfully puts it on his
shoulders and goes home.* Luke 15:5, *NIV*

Last summer I had a preaching engagement at the
Tabernacle in Ocean City, New Jersey. My hotel room
overlooked the Atlantic and the busy boardwalk which
parallels the seaside. Thousands of people stroll or ride
bicycles along the boardwalk and frequent the famous .
saltwater taffy shops or the amusement parks situated
along the way.

From my room I could see the endless streams of
people walking aimlessly. A blend of clattering voices and
the carnival sounds of the merry-go-round wafted into my
room on the soft, salty, humid, summer night's breeze. A
pleasant background for my time of study in preparation
for my sermon the next day. My mind was focused on
Luke 15 and Jesus' parables of the lost sheep and the lost

coin. I did not expect that what I was about to hear over one of the speakers which adorn the light posts along the boardwalk would bring what I was reading about into stark reality.

Piercing through the din was an anonymous announcement. None of the people on the boardwalk seemed to hear, respond or care. But from my vantage the words were alarming, though the announcer's voice did not express the pathos and anguish of the distress.

"A little girl about five years old, answering to the name of Wendy, has been lost. She is wearing a yellow dress and carrying a teddy bear. She has brown eyes, auburn hair. Anyone knowing the whereabouts of Wendy, please report to the Music Pier. Her parents are waiting for her here."

I tried to return to my reading. But my mind was on Wendy. Who was she? Where was she now in what must have looked to her to be a forest of legs along the boardwalk? How did she feel without the clasp of her father's strong hand? I felt heart-wrenching empathy as I pictured her clutching her faithful teddy bear, tears streaming down her face, her heart bursting with fright and loneliness.

Then I pictured her parents. That triggered my own parental concerns and flooded me with memories of times my own children had gotten lost. I wanted to start a search party all my own, or go wait with the parents. What must they be feeling? Imagine all the tragic things that could happen to Wendy: the sea, physical harm, strangers...

I was deeply relieved when I learned that Wendy was found. I pictured the thankful looks of love on the parents' faces and felt the joy they must have expressed. Warmth pulsated in my arms as I almost felt the tenderness of holding sobbing, little Wendy. I could hear something inside me saying, "It's alright now, Wendy. Don't cry anymore. It's okay. We've found you. Never let go of my hand again. I love you, Wendy."

Then I looked out of my window again at the streams of humanity along the boardwalk. How many of them were lost and did not know it? Or how many felt a deep lostness inside and wished an announcement would be made about their spiritual condition? Did anyone care? I wondered how many of them knew that they needed a heavenly Father as much as Wendy needed her daddy.

Father, thank you for your love and for the promise that when you take us in your arms we need not be lost anymore! Amen.

Adapted from the book *Autobiography of God* by Lloyd John Ogilvie. Copyright 1979 by Regal Books, a division of Gospel Light Publications, Ventura, CA. Used by permission.

O Those Lilies

Lawrence A. Tucker

*I am the resurrection and the life....whoever lives
and believes in me will never die.*
John 11:25-26, *NIV*

One hot, stifling, humid August morning we stood
with our family and friends as a kindly pastor spoke
words of comfort and committed the body of our young
son to the ground.

We lingered a while looking at the floral pieces
covering the small grave. Heavy of heart, lonely in spirit,
we returned to our parents' home. In unremitting heat, the
day passed. As evening's shadows began to creep across
the grave, we returned to sit a few minutes by the resting
place of our son.

The floral tributes, so proud and erect in the morning,
were now all wilted — ruined by the heat. Their
drooping leaves and shattered blooms were matched by
the brokenness of our hearts. With such little warning our
son was gone, our arms were empty.

As we sat quietly, our eyes were drawn to the central

floral piece. Parts of it had paid the price demanded by the heat. But not all. Out of the center of a wilted background, twelve white calla lilies stood straight and erect, undaunted by the circumstances of the day. They had not been overwhelmed by scorching heat. In the midst of the dead and dying they had lived. Why?

Probing the structure of the piece, I freed a bloom. The secret became known. The stem of the bloom was fastened in a small vial of water. When all elements combined to destroy their beauty, the callas had a source of inner strength. By that strength they had continued to live in beauty, with a promise of hope.

Joining hands we drew comfort from a source almost pushed aside by our grief. Had the Master not said, "I am the resurrection and the life. He who believes in me will live, even though he dies, and whoever lives and believes in me will never die"? In that moment we received inner strength from our living Lord.

Thank God for the calla lilies and their message to us that day.

Father of all who sorrow, give us the assurance of your presence now and in the life to come. Amen.

Capturing Our Thought Life

Edward L. Hayes

As he thinks within himself, so he is.
Proverbs 23:7, *NASB*

Our thoughts shape our character. The inner anatomy of our soul reveals the true spiritual condition. Inner deceit or lust is as evil as a criminal act.

Thoughts, we say, are private. No one gets arrested for thinking evil. The domain of the mind is private turf. As long as we act civilly, no one can charge us with wrong behavior.

This line of reasoning is deceptive. It is a tragic delusion of the mind. It legitimizes hypocrisy.

Jesus said there is a link between thought and action. "You have heard that it was said, 'You shall not commit adultery'; but I say to you, that anyone who looks on a woman to lust for her has committed adultery with her already in his heart'" (Matthew 5:27-28). The thought is tantamount to the act.

I have reflected on my own thought life and have often wondered about its uncontrollable nature. Sometimes I feel it is like an untamed river rushing down a path of destruction. Unchecked it could wipe out a reputation, ruin a career, hurt people badly.

The Bible places blame for this condition on the fact that our minds have been blinded by the god of this world (2 Corinthians 4:4). Satan is the deceiver. His stronghold includes the human mind. In fact, that may be the real battleground where spiritual warfare takes place.

God looks on the thoughts and intents of the heart. He is not fooled by outward conformity to propriety and social custom. "The Lord knows the thoughts of man" (Psalm 94:11).

The Bible calls for a renewal of our minds. It appeals to the level of conscience and the exercise of the human will. Though blinded by sin and marred by the Adamic fall, the mind can be transformed by the saving grace of God. To believe in one's heart is to bring our thoughts under the lordship of Jesus Christ.

Personal salvation does not liberate the mind from evil thoughts. It is a daily battle. The fortress of the mind, under the new management of the indwelling Spirit can be brought into captivity to Christ. This is what Paul declared in 2 Corinthians 10:5: "We are taking every thought captive to the obedience of Christ." The battle for the mind is won at the foot of the Cross. Daily surrender to Christ is our only defense against the ravages of an undisciplined mind.

There is also a very practical way to capture the mind. We are given a road map in Philippians 4:8: "Whatever is true, whatever is honorable, whatever is right, whatever is pure, whatever is lovely, whatever is of good repute, if there is any excellence and if anything worthy of praise, let your mind dwell on these things." Focused thoughts are the best guarantee of inner purity of mind.

I want my thoughts to be acceptable in your sight, O Lord, my rock and my redeemer. Amen.

Anytime, Anyplace!

Leif A. Tangvald

*Where two or three have gathered in My name,
there I am in their midst.* Matthew 18:20, *NASB*

A college dorm. Noise. People. Laughter. Parties.
Fun. Stereos. Pressure to fit in. Sometimes a college dorm
room can seem far removed from the house of the Lord.

But it needn't be.

One night not too long ago, my friends Brian and Pee
Wee were studying with me for a test. Somehow we
steered the discussion into the topic of the second coming
of Christ. I reached for my Bible, and we entered into a
five-hour marathon study on the book of Revelation.

We argued. We read. We laughed. We explored. But
most of all, I think we *grew* in knowledge and
understanding of God's Word.

I'm not sure we solved any of the major questions of
theology that night. And we didn't do too well on our test

the next day. But it did prove to me that opportunities to study and share God's Word can happen anytime, anyplace—even very late in a college dorm room.

Lord, thank you for being available to me— anytime, anyplace! Amen.

Surviving an Earthquake

James E. Bolton

Only unshakable things will be left.
Hebrews 12:27, *TLB*

During a major earthquake, everything for hundreds of miles is severely shaken. The jerking and shaking motion of the earth creates such enormous stresses that it quickly tears most buildings to pieces. Only the strongest and best-anchored buildings survive such a thrashing.

Likewise, our personal world can be shaken like an earthquake when we lose our job, a loved one, or some valued possession. Such losses can create enormous stresses in our lives. And when they do, we need to have a strong anchor to keep us from being torn to pieces.

That strong anchor is Jesus Christ. When we listen to Him and let Him control our lives, then we can "be compared to a wise man, who built his house upon the rock. And the rain descended, the floods came and the winds blew, and burst against that house, yet it did not fall, for it had been founded upon the rock" (Matthew 7:24-25, *NASB*).

Just as the strong and well-anchored buildings are able to survive earthquakes, when we are well-anchored to the rock of Jesus Christ, we can survive the earthquake-like problems that come against us.

Dear Jesus, help me to be so securely anchored in you that I will have the strength and wisdom to overcome the problems that come my way. Amen.

Get It Together

Ray Ortlund

*We ought always to thank God for you, brothers,
and rightly so, because your faith is growing more
and more, and the love every one of you has for
each other is increasing.* 2 Thessalonians 1:3, *NIV*

"The Lone Ranger rides again!" But not in the
Christian life and ministry. The rugged individualist is not
the characteristic hero of the New Testament.

No way. You hunt for loners — and you never find
any. Even the above words to the Thessalonians didn't
come from one sender, but three: Paul, Silas, and
Timothy. The words were Paul's, by the Spirit, but he had
a team of godly guys surrounding him.

And think about the life-style you see in the New
Testament. Jesus had the *seventy,* who were His team in
ministry; He had the *twelve;* and out of the twelve He had
a particular *three.* You seldom find Him alone. Mark 3:14
says He called His disciples "that they might be with Him,"
this One whose name is Immanuel — "God with us"
(Matthew 1:23).

And Paul never went solo. Whatever he was doing he had an entourage at his elbow. That's how others learned and grew, and eventually replaced him. And how he loved his close brothers: "We have the same Holy Spirit," he wrote about his team-member, Titus, "and we walk in each other's steps, doing things the same way" (2 Corinthians 12:18, *TLB*).

Do you have a Titus, a Timothy, a Silas? Do a few others share your dreams and your burdens, your sins and your victories? Do you feel accountable to them, and responsible for them? Are you discipling younger men in Christ? Are you discipled by someone who's walked with Him longer than you?

If you're typical, you're a "friendless American male," so inhibited and bottled up inside that you can only act macho and talk news-sports-and-weather. That's not only silly, superficial, and frustrating, it's unbiblical. God never planned for you to be a loner — and lonely.

Hey, even the Lone Ranger had Tonto!

Take off you mask. Move into the lives of a few others and share your heart. Meet weekly with four or five brothers, and get to know each other deeply. I've done this for about twenty years now, and I'm loved! I'm prayed for! I'm challenged!

Lord, thank you for the examples in your Word that show I am not to go through life alone and lonely. Bring people into my life today, people to whom I can give love and by whom I can feel loved. Amen.

I Keep Forgetting

Robert Beckwith

Bless the Lord, O my soul, and forget none of His benefits. Psalm 103:2, *NASB*

Soon after posting a notice for a couple of roommates on the bulletin board of my new school, one position was quickly filled. But I still needed another roommate to help keep my expenses down.

Not too long afterward, I received a phone call from another student by the name of Ramon. He was foreign and must have had a speech impediment, for he was hard to understand. But we did manage to discuss a few things, and the next day we went together to the apartment manager's office for Ramon's interview.

Normally, the interview was merely a formality. But in this case, it was obvious from the beginning that his application would not be accepted. I have to admit I was somewhat relieved when the management said they needed more time to review his credit.

Ramon was noticeably disappointed, but, apparently, rejection was not something new to him. I felt bad for him and offered to drive him to the bus stop. On the way, he shared some of his unhappiness with me and told how he tried to be a good person and attend church as much as possible. But somehow none of that seemed to make any difference, he explained.

This then afforded me the opportunity to share my faith with him. As I explained my personal relationship with Christ and what He's done in my life, I sensed God at work. And after our short drive I could see that my new friend was at least somewhat encouraged.

In trying to express his thanks for my help, Ramon began talking very quickly. Much of what he was saying was not understandable, but what did come out loud and clear was "Your generosity I keep forgetting."

I appreciated his "compliment," but later what he said hit me with a different meaning. It was sobering when I considered how many times I had forgotten, or not even recognized, God's daily blessings in my life. Had I really considered God's generosity?

Then I remembered His words in Psalm 103:2: "Bless the Lord, O my soul, and forget none of His benefits."

It's challenging to recognize the generosity from above, but more of a responsibility to forget not one benefit.

Holy God, you have been and continue to be so generous. You gave the ultimate gift, Jesus Christ. In the busyness of my daily life, help me to always remember your many blessings. Amen.

Confidence that's Unshakable

Herman D. Rosenberger

Therefore do not cast away your confidence.
Hebrews 10:35, *NKJV*

Motorists weaving through the gentle hills, pine forests, and back roads north of Marshall, Texas, will happen on a sign that says: "This is Uncertain, Texas, Home of Caddo Lake, Population 176."

Some say the name, Uncertain, dates back to the days of steamboat travel when the water level varied so greatly that no one was certain that they could get in and back out again. Others say the name seemed appropriate since paddle boat pilots often became confused by the many arms leading off the channel up to Jefferson, Texas. Still others believe the name derives from the uncertainty of ownership of the land that is now called Uncertain. Though the actual origin of the name is not known, it is, to say the least, a unique and curious one.

There are many uncertainties in this world: the weather, the stock market, the length of our days on earth, and what the future holds for us. Because of these uncertainties, we are sometimes faced with unexpected events that threaten to shake our confidence.

The writer of Hebrews exhorts us not to cast away our confidence. Unlike the steamboat travelers who were uncertain as to whether they would make it in and out of the area because of varying water levels, we have confidence that wherever the Lord leads us, we will be safe. For He has promised never to leave us or forsake us (Hebrews 13:5). And, unlike the pilots of the boats who were often uncertain about which course they should follow, we have perfect confidence in the One who said, "I am the way" (John 14:6).

Thank you, Lord, that in the midst of the uncertainties of life, I have the confidence that you are with me, and that you will never leave me or forsake me. Amen.

But God!

Bob Baker

O Lord, how many are my foes! How many rise up against me! Many are saying of me, "God will not deliver him." But you are a shield around me, O Lord; my Glorious One, who lifts up my head.
Psalm 3:1-3, *NIV*

"What's that he gave you?" "Why, it's a bullet — a silver bullet!" "Who *was* that masked man?"

Then a sound of thundering hoofbeats, a cry of "Hi-Yo-Silver!" and the closing strains of the *William Tell Overture*.

No doubt, the Lone Ranger was one of the truly great interventionists. He, with his faithful Indian companion, Tonto, intervened for truth and justice all over the western half of radio-land.

Has anyone passed you any silver bullets lately? Does anyone intervene like that in real life?

David wrote Psalm 3 when he was fleeing for his life from his son, Absalom. A refugee king running from home and friends because his life was at risk from his own

71

son — and anyone else who thought him fair game.

David cries out: "How many are my foes! How many rise up against me!" David, after years of kingship, finds that the old enemies are still there. Those who were not pursuing David were chanting taunts about God's defection from the king. "Many are saying of me, 'God will not deliver him.'" What a predicament. David feels forsaken by man and God.

Yet what beautiful words of intervention are next. "But, you, Lord..." Yes, God can intervene!

This is one of six times that God's Word gives us these words of intervention and hope — "But, God."

God will intervene in the most desperate moments of life. Here David describes God as a shield covering him on every side and the one who can lift his head when bowed down with shame.

In the moment of our greatest need, God stands — all around us — as the encircling one, the shield. And as He stands close to us, it's as if He puts two gentle fingers under our chin to lift our drooping head and says, "Look up — at me."

No silver bullets, no hoofbeats from a great white stallion, no inspiring music — but the real and living God, covering us on every side and lifting our head to look into His eyes.

Father, you step into my life just when I need you. Lift my head so I can clearly see you. Amen.

Infrequent Flier

Tony Sbrana

*So from now on we regard no one from a worldly
point of view. Though we once regarded Christ in
this way, we do so no longer. Therefore, if anyone is
in Christ, he is a new creation; the old has gone, the
new has come!* 2 Corinthians 5:16-17, *NIV*

Many businesses these days frequently require
employees to fly. Not mine. And maybe that's one reason
I love flying so much. I mean, let's face it, repetition is the
novocaine of life.

But there's something that happens to me when I'm up
in an airplane. I look out, down, miles back or ahead, and
I feel the wonder of knowing I'm seeing things from a
perspective that, for most of human history, was reserved
for God and His angels. Truly a "heavenly" perspective.
And I'm reminded that, with the Lord of heaven living in
my heart, I can opt to see from that perspective all the
time.

The young executive across the aisle from me drums
an efficient tattoo on his lap-top computer. He's wearing a

fashionable pair of reading glasses. A stewardess glances at me with her striking blue orbs and I realize she's wearing tinted contacts. Both have made good choices.

But a far better choice is available to me...infinitely better than simply choosing among frames or lenses. I have a choice of *eyes!* I can actually lower my eyelids, utter a prayer, and lift them again to find I'm looking out through the supernatural eyes of God. Talk about improved depth perception! My old eyes saw mountains as daunting and formidable. My new eyes, from their heavenly perspective, see mountains as interesting little ripples in the earth's surface. My old eyes saw people as confusing and potentially troublesome. My new eyes see them as uniformly needy — and beloved.

We touch down without incident and taxi to the terminal. I step outside into the cool evening air and gaze upward. It looks like rain. But through new eyes I see the storm from the other side, and suddenly the impending downpour doesn't seem threatening at all.

I really do love flying.

Lord, grant me your perspective on the people and situations I encounter each day. Grant me the courage, boldness, perseverance, and especially the love that only comes when, by the power of the Holy Spirit, I see through your eyes. Amen.

A Man of Character

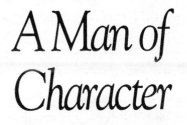

Mark McLean

*Behold, I, having examined him [Jesus] before you,
have found no fault in this man.* Luke 23:14, *KJV*

Whatever happened to qualities like integrity,
honesty, determination, courage, and dependability?
Why, in this day of situation ethics, is it so hard to find
people who never waver in their character, who never let
down "just this once"?

The old saying goes: A good man is hard to find. And it
becomes truer as the days go by. Worst of all is when
Christians fail to have integrity in their businesses and
personal dealings, because even the worldliest non-
Christian expects honesty and dependability from those
who call themselves Christians.

Maybe we need to take stock of our priorities and ask:
Whose life is it anyway? God's Word continually drives
home the point that, if we are Christians, our lives are not

to be lived for ourselves anymore, but for Him who loved us and bought us by His blood.

In 1 Corinthians 6:19-20, the Apostle Paul reminds us of God's ownership of us: "What? Know ye not that your body is the temple of the Holy Ghost which is in you, which ye have of God, and ye are not your own? For ye are bought with a price: Therefore glorify God in your body, and in your spirit which are God's."

What could be more glorifying to God than to have His children behave in such a manner as to be a testimony to the world He desires so desperately to save? At one time or another, we have all seen the powerful presence of a godly man of integrity and moral character. No one ignores him; people are either drawn by his strength or despise him for the conviction he brings merely by his presence. Either way, he is being a light where he is, simply by his ability to stand up and be counted for God.

Lord, help me to be a godly example wherever you put me today. Give me the strength and courage to follow you in an uncompromising way, and to be your light in my world. Amen.

The High Way
to Faith

Al Munger

*So faith comes from hearing, and hearing by the
word of Christ.* Romans 10:17, *NASB*

It was a narrow, two-lane road twisting through the
hills toward Mazatlan, Mexico. The trucks were slow and
traffic was backing up.

Our friends, Betty and Joe, had just piloted their motor
home around a big truck that was coughing diesel smoke.
Now it was our turn to pass this monster. A dozen
impatient drivers were behind us. *CURVA PELIGROSA*
(Dangerous Curve) the sign warned. We could only see
about one hundred and fifty feet ahead before the road
disappeared around the mountain, but I decided to go for
it. Shifting into second gear, I put the pedal to the floor
and we started around the truck.

The drivers behind us must have thought we were
crazy. An oncoming bus or truck would scatter us all over

the landscape. But they didn't know that just seconds before we started to pass, Betty had called us on the CB radio saying, "The road is clear for half a mile." The move that appeared suicidal was safe because our friends could see the road ahead and knew there were no cars coming. I chose to believe Betty. I knew she wouldn't lie to me.

Isn't that what faith is — believing someone enough to make a decision and act on it? "Now faith is the assurance of things hoped for, the conviction of things not seen" (Hebrews 11:1). How do we obtain faith? The Bible also says, "Faith comes from hearing, and hearing by the word of Christ."

From the human perspective the road ahead can be unknown and dangerous. But when we choose to believe God's Word and listen for the still small voice of the Holy Spirit, we can proceed with confidence and safety. Our Father God will not lie to us and He sees the future that is hidden to us. The "high way" to faith is simply hearing and depending on His Word.

Jesus, plant your Word deep in my convictions that I might trust you more in those dangerous decisions of life. Thank you for being so patient with me. Amen.

Working Up
a Thirst

Glenn W. Hoerr

*As the deer pants for the water brooks, so my soul
pants for Thee, O God. My soul thirsts for God, for
the living God.* Psalm 42:1-2, *NASB*

During my high school and college years, I enjoyed
playing soccer. No, that's an understatement. I thrived on
the game!

In fact, I played all year round wherever I could, no
matter what the conditions. Since I lived in the east, that
meant freezing cold in the winter and heat and humidity
in the summer. It didn't matter, though, because I loved
playing soccer.

Each year, however, that love was tested greatly. As the
new school year approached, I faced the dreaded two-a-
day workouts, which included a three-hour practice
session in the morning and another two- to three-hour
session in the afternoon. The heat was always in the

nineties and the humidity was always high. When the constant running drills, contact, and verbal prodding from the coach were added, two things resulted. Sincere questions about my commitment to the game would arise, and second, a deep thirst, due too the heat, would develop. My mouth and throat would be dry, I would feel lightheaded, and my legs were like rubber all at the same time. No matter how much we had run, or how tired I was I always seemed to be able to run in from the field, though, because I knew that I had a half-gallon of Gatorade on ice in the locker room to quench my thirst. After my thirst was satisfied, I was more than willing to go back out into the heat and do it all over again.

As I proceed through life, I encounter numerous circumstances, concerns, and questions that leave me feeling thirsty. And that's when I ask myself: Will I satisfy the thirst by my own devices, or will I satisfy the thirst by seeking God more fully? For only as I drink of the water He provides in His Word, and in prayer with Him, will I be truly satisfied, and ready to go out and "do it all over again."

Father, help me to pursue you in such a way that I create a continual thirst and find satisfaction only from you. Amen.

A Spiritual Inheritance

Wes Haystead

*A good man leaves an inheritance to his children's
children.* Proverbs 13:22, *NASB*

When my dad died, I grieved for what my children
had lost. I grieved that Kari, my daughter, had grown up
far away from him, although they had always had a very
special relationship. I grieved that Dad died when my
sons, Andrew and Jonathan, were so young that in years
to come their memories of him would be fleeting. I
wanted my children to know him as I had, to grow up
with his blend of enthusiasm, compassion, and wisdom.

What I wanted was for him to keep on being Dad to
me and to them. I wanted him to be available to model
those qualities I admire but often find hard to
demonstrate. I found myself wondering if the inheritance
Dad had left would ever reach my kids. Or would I be the

klutz who couldn't pass it on?

Then every once in awhile I hear my dad's words coming out of my mouth, and I realize that a great deal of who he was is still a part of me. I repeat his jokes (my kids call them dumb — just as I used to do). I use his clichés (the same ones he claimed were from his father). I offer his advice (which I did not always follow). And I get a sense of how Dad's heritage of values and beliefs and personality are helping me to pass on that inheritance.

My awareness of how Dad's influence remains a part of me adds to my understanding of how my heavenly Father is also with me as I seek to pass on a spiritual heritage to my children. There's a very real sense in which much that my children see of God they see in me. Not just when I pray or read the Bible or teach Sunday School. But when I rub Jonathan's back at bedtime, or read aloud *Bears in the Night* for the umpteenth time, while I pitch and then chase the old tennis balls that Andrew slams past me, while I help Kari move her things into her college apartment...I find myself thinking that I'm getting a chance to demonstrate a little bit of my heavenly Father's unbounded love.

And at those times when I'm impatient or unkind, I realize afresh how much I need God's presence in my life — and I toss a little blame Dad's way since he wasn't perfect, either.

Please, heavenly Father, help me today to add something of eternal value to the inheritance of my children. Amen.

Watch Out for Those Little Foxes

Ray Beeson

Catch the foxes for us, the little foxes that are ruining the vineyards, while our vineyards are in blossom. Song of Solomon 2:15, *NASB*

King Solomon wrote about foxes. He noted that it was the little ones that spoiled the vines.

I love the outdoors, but I don't know a great deal about foxes. If I were asked to consider that they were a nuisance in some situation, I would assume that the bigger the fox the more the danger.

Recently, the word *little* has caught my attention. In many, if not most, of the major issues and problems of life, it has been a little thing that has caused the most difficulty. For example, I'm aware of a man who neglected a little problem at home until it caused untold pain in his marriage. He knew it was there but was so concerned about the big things in life that the smaller issue eventually spoiled his relationship with his wife.

Little foxes, what are they? For some, they could be thoughts. Have you ever sat in church and wondered, what am I doing here? This isn't doing me one bit of good? Or, after a disappointment or personal failure, you think, what's the use, it's just not possible to please God. Maybe in regards to a commitment or vow, you've thought, this isn't really what I wanted to do. Mere thoughts, maybe. But they can lead to problems if not controlled.

For others, little foxes are the moments when they let down, just slightly, in what they know to be ethical and appropriate — like an intimate conversation with a secretary over a cup of coffee, an incorrect statement on an income tax form, a conversation in which the accuracy is somewhat debatable. It's amazing how far things can get out of hand for people who never meant for anything to go wrong.

Should we try to kill all those little foxes? Probably not. Most of us have been hunting the big ones long enough to know that no matter how many we deal with, more just keep showing up.

The only real solution involves putting a guard around the vineyards of our hearts. And Jesus has sent the Holy Spirit to be that guard. The Old Testament law tried to kill the little foxes with its "thou shalt not" approach. But that was only a temporary measure until Christ came.

Mankind needed something better than an outward moral code to solve our problems. We needed a change from within. And this change can only come by the infilling of the Spirit of God. Only then will those little foxes that seek to enter into the vineyards of our hearts be held at bay.

Heavenly Father, I'm aware of the little foxes that would love to get in to cause me difficulties and problems. I'm also aware that a daily portion of the Holy Spirit is what I need to be my guard. Fill me this day anew. Amen.

A Slice of Life

James L. Snyder

*And we know that all things work together for good
to them that love God, to them who are the called
according to his purpose.* Romans 8:28, *KJV*

Recently I stopped by a local restaurant and ordered
a piece of coconut cream pie and cup of coffee. Now that,
in itself, is not unusual or significant. But sitting there
having my dessert, I thought how that piece of pie
represents life in general.

A piece of pie is not a singular thing. Any cook worth
his or her salt will tell you there are many ingredients that
go into the making of a pie. Besides the ingredients, time
is necessary to prepare and bake the pie.

If we were to lay out the ingredients of a coconut
cream pie, they would not be tempting in the least. But it's
not the individual parts, but the combination of those
parts that make up the pie. And the proper blend of all the
ingredients is so important. Too much of any one
ingredient will throw the whole thing off balance and ruin
a good pie.

Life also consists of many ingredients. And the proper blend of those ingredients makes life exciting and fulfilling. When there's too much of one thing, even if it's good, all of life will seem out of balance.

At times, we encounter a particular ingredient in life that we don't like or appreciate. An injustice, physical pain, the loss of a family member or job. In and of itself, this particular ingredient is not appealing, but blended with the rest of our life experiences, it will add balance and proper perspective.

Just as the cook is combining ingredients to give us a beautiful and tasty dessert, so is our heavenly Father blending the ingredients of our lives to make us into what pleases Him and serves His purpose and will for our lives.

He has the perfect recipe!

Oh, God, forgive me when I balk at certain ingredients added to my life. I give you the right to make of me what you will, for I trust in the knowledge that all things work together for my ultimate good. Amen.

He's a Loving Father

Josh McDowell

*For all have sinned and fall short of the glory of
God, being justified as a gift by His grace through
the redemption which is in Christ Jesus; whom God
displayed publicly as a propitiation in His blood
through faith.* Romans 3:23-25, *NASB*

Often I ask people the question, "For whom did
Jesus die?" and usually they reply, "For me," or "For the
world." And I'll say, "Yes, that's right, but for whom else
did Jesus die?" and usually they'll say, "Why, I don't
know." I reply, "For God the Father."

You see, Christ not only died for us but He also died
for the Father. This is described in Romans 3 where it talks
about propitiation. Propitiation basically means

satisfaction of a requirement. And when Jesus died on the cross, He not only died for us but He died to meet the holy and just requirements of the basic nature of God.

An incident that took place several years ago in California illuminates what Jesus did on the cross in order to solve the problem God had in dealing with the sin of humanity. A young woman was picked up for speeding. She was ticketed and taken before the judge. The judge read off the citation and said, "Guilty or not guilty?" The woman replied, "Guilty." The judge brought down the gavel and fined her $100 or ten days.

Then an amazing thing took place. The judge stood up, took off his robe, walked down around in front, took out his billfold, and paid the fine. What's the explanation of this? The judge was her father. He loved his daughter, yet he was a just judge. His daughter had broken the law and he couldn't simply say to her, "Because I love you so much, I forgive you. You may leave." If he had done that, he wouldn't have been a righteous judge. He wouldn't have upheld the law. But he loved his daughter so much that he was willing to take off his judicial robe and come down in front and represent her as her father and pay the fine.

This illustration pictures to some extent what God did for us through Jesus Christ. We sinned. The Bible says, "The wages of sin is death." No matter how much He loved us, God had to bring down the gavel and say *death,* because He is a righteous and just God. And yet, being a loving God, He loved us so much that He was willing to come down off the throne in the form of the man Christ Jesus and pay the price for us, which was Christ's death on the cross.

O Lord, we sinned, but you paid the price. What a loving Father you are. Amen.

Act Your Age!

David H. Hepburn

*Fathers, do not exasperate your children; instead,
bring them up in the training and instruction of the
Lord.* Ephesians 6:4, *NIV*

Supervising student teachers was one of my happier
assignments while I taught high school. However, I must
admit, I would shudder when one of these aspiring tutors
would tell a frustrated student to "act your age." That was
the problem, the student was acting his age. Becoming a
teacher is a learning process, and so is becoming an adult
and a father.

We are in big trouble if we have learned how to father
from the television imagery. Fatherhood doesn't run in
one-hour segments with commercial breaks. Fatherhood
cannot be turned off when interest is running low.
Fatherhood is full-time, long-term commitment.

There are those moments — when little Davey has
broken the neighbor's window, or little Betsy tried to give
the cat a bath in the toilet — when we wish we could
take a commercial break. Perhaps the situation is even

worse: a son or daughter has been caught stealing or with drugs in their possession. How do we handle situations like these?

God's Word admonishes, "When I became a man, I put childish ways behind me" (1 Corinthians 13:11), and for us to retaliate in anger would be childish. Instead we must seek to capture the opportunity of the moment for training and instruction in the Lord. After all, having been adolescents once ourselves, we should know how they feel. What a difference when we have grown up and realize they cannot know how we feel. Men, the ball's in our court!

My father found such an opportunity for training when I was in serious trouble at age sixteen. Somehow, after the policeman left our home, my father saw past the hurt and embarrassment and assured me of his forgiveness. The experience was put away "as far as the east is from the west" and never mentioned again. When I became an adult, I discovered that my father had taught me — during that teachable moment — an important lesson on how to become a forgiving father. I felt loved, not exasperated. Dad was so in line with Scripture.

Lord, give me spiritual eyes to see our children as you see them, and wisdom to recognize those special opportunities that might come wrapped up in pain. Amen.

Every Talent Counts

Dick Hagerman

His master replied, "Well done, good and faith
servant! You have been faithful with a few things."
Matthew 25:21, *NIV*

She wore a plain blue housedress and dark shoes,
and her dull blond hair was tied in a bun above her collar.
When she stepped into the front of the bus, I remembered
her. I had been away from my home church for eight
years, but I couldn't forget her shyness. One-on-one
contact had been difficult for her.

A quiet smile of recognition crossed both our faces as
she walked to the back of the bus.

I wondered why she had boarded and where she was
going.

Ten miles later, my questions were answered. As she
walked off the bus at the next stop, she placed a piece of
folded paper on each unoccupied seat. I picked up one of

the papers and read about Christ's salvation, and how to obtain this gift of God.

I thought: So this is how she witnesses for her Savior. She knows the excitement of a daily walk with Christ. Yet shyness prevents a one-on-one evangelism. She is zealous, thankful, and caring, and is using a talent God gave her to share Christ's love with others.

I knew that when she returned home she would again leave the tracts and pray that the Holy Spirit would touch those who read them.

"Well done, good and faithful servant."

Dear Lord, let me use the talent you've given me to share Christ's love with someone today. Amen.

Tipping the Hat to God

Robert E. Osman

*Give, and it will be given to you; good measure,
pressed down, shaken together, running over, will
be put into your lap. For the measure you give will
be the measure you get back.* Luke 6:38, *RSV*

I remember as a young boy how the transients and
drunks congregated on the steps of the Roman Catholic
Church in the center of my hometown. I also noticed that
they always tipped their hat to the church as they passed
by.

It was much later that I read that the avowed atheist
and philosopher Nietzsche always did the same. He never
passed the church without tipping his hat. He didn't go in;
he only made the gesture. In his thinking, his action may
have constituted a sort of insurance, as if to say, just in
case there was a God he wanted it on record that he had
not been entirely indifferent.

95

Even as Christians and church members we so often respond in the same way. The stewardship challenge of giving of our time and talents brings a figurative tipping of the hat to God. It involves no wrestling with conviction or conscience. So many give just a little of self in the same way they buy group hospitalization. Though they are sure that God is on their side, "A little insurance never hurt anybody."

I went into the Navy as a chaplain because of a challenge made by a minister to my congregation, and not necessarily intended for me. He said, "You do not have any right to hear the gospel twice until everyone in the world has heard it once." He used the illustration of Christ feeding the five thousand. Suppose He fed only the first three rows, then turned around and started all over again?

I used to encourage young people to give themselves for full-time ministry as pastors or missionaries. Now I preach that every Christian should be a minister for God every day, wherever he or she may be.

Are you feeling empty, unfulfilled? Maybe you need to ask yourself: Am I only tipping my hat to God? God's Word says that the measure you give is the measure you will receive. The more you give, the more you will get in return: blessings that can't even be measured.

Lord, help me to be real. I don't want to merely tip my hat to you. I want to take it off in deep faith! Amen.

Teamwork and Tennis Shoes

Michael B. Reynolds

*Trust in the Lord with all your heart and lean not
on your own understanding; in all your ways
acknowledge him, and he will make your paths
straight.* Proverbs 3:5-6, *NIV*

My son's tennis shoes are always in one of two
places: on his feet or lost. There is no in-between.
Searches begin under his bed in the bedroom, then
behind the hamper in the bathroom, under the
newspapers in the living room, and on to the washer in
the utility room.

Of course, he always conducts these searches by lying
flat on his back with his legs and feet held in mid-air.
Paralyzed from the trauma, he shouts ideas of where the
tennies might be, if only Mom or Dad would look there.

It is certainly natural for a child to depend on Mom and
Dad for a lot of things, and helping each other find lost

97

items is part of it. But many of the best searches as a family are done as a team. It teaches responsibility and cooperation and avoids the "spoiling" effect of a parents-only search.

As believers we call upon God for many answers in life, some of which do require divine insight. But often our answers come as we search with Him as a team. Acknowledging Him in our ways is more than uttering a prayer. It is a way of searching, of reviewing the options and considering our actions with a perspective not entirely our own. It's God's mind networking with ours that reveals many answers and determines the paths we need to take.

There certainly are times when we find ourselves flat on our backs and our only solution is to call upon God. Many routine things in life, however, are solved on our feet.

Whether God's guidance is by circumstance or insight, teamwork is the most successful approach.

Lord, help me not to take your guidance for granted. Rather help me to be a strong participant in the search for your pathways. Amen.

Now That's Persistence!

Dan Driver

*But as for you, continue in what you have learned
and have become convinced of, because you
know those from whom you learned it.*
2 Timothy 3:14, *NIV*

During his boyhood, Sir Winston Churchill attended Harrow, a boy's boarding school. After becoming Great Britain's prime minister during World War II, he went back to his alma mater to speak.

The school headmaster gave the boys pen and paper to write down his words. Sir Winston Churchill's speech to the boys that day consisted of these words: Never give in. Never! Never! Never!

The path of the Christian life is oftentimes difficult to follow. Obstacles will get in our way. Because of who we follow, however, we are to adopt a life-style of commitment.

Most people are able to understand and accept this. They respect a person's commitment to a cause. This is what we must exhibit in our Christian lives, commitment to Christ. But there are those who enjoy putting down this type of commitment.

Once I had a supervisor who ragged me continually about my commitment to Christ. One day he told me that my life's priorities weren't right at all and what I needed was a "night out with the boys." I declined to follow his advice, which further upset him. From that day on, our relationship has gone downhill.

Another time my supervisor ridiculed the Bible and all religious faith. Anyone who believed and displayed any faith at all were "sissies" in his eyes. They weren't "real people."

No, living the Christian life is never easy. Circumstances and individuals can make it a difficult path to follow.

But because of what lies ahead for every believer, we must never give in to those who would desire to defeat us and the One in whom we trust. We can, however, with the strength Christ gives us, continue to press on. We need *never* give in.

Dear God, help me to remember what I have learned about you and have become convinced of. Allow me to remain confident of you and committed to following your path. Amen.

Welcome Home

Donald L. Evans, Jr.

*"For this son of mine was dead and is alive again;
he was lost and is found." So they began to
celebrate.* Luke 15:24, *NIV*

I needed to get away. I had some hard thinking to do.
It's always been my practice to find seclusion when I have
a tough problem to think through.

My problem was guilt. Although I had grown up with
Jesus, I walked away from Him sometime in my high
school years. College and graduate school found me
hungry to study comparative religions and philosophy,
always searching for meaning in life. Now, through the
urging of the Spirit, and the prayers of my family, I
realized the truth. The answer had been mine, but I had
turned my back on Him. I felt sick. How could I look
Jesus in the face? How could He accept me again after the
way I had treated Him? Maybe a mini-vacation would
help me sort it all out.

I set out for a distant mountain lake, a place I hadn't
visited since my youth. The lake had always been a

favorite spot for me, but now uncertainty loomed. I had heard of developments and logging in the area. Would the lake be as I remembered it?

As my truck crested the ridge and began descending into the lake's basin, my fears dissipated. All was as it had been. Trees, shoreline, fishing, and camping areas were just as I remembered. The lake sparkled at me and I knew I was welcome once again.

I lifted the heavy tent from the pickup and almost dropped it as the light flashed on inside my head. Jesus' love for me is constant and unchanging. I thought of the prodigal son, and my surroundings drove home the point. Reassured, I asked Him in again, and the wind in the trees whispered, "Welcome home!"

Gracious Lord, thanks for being so unchanging. Thanks for your readiness to welcome me home whether I've strayed from you for a minute or for years. Amen.

Close Calls or Celebrations?

W. Terry Whalin

*Spread your protection over them, that those
who love your name may rejoice in you.*
Psalm 5:11, *NIV*

Traffic zipped steadily along the freeway that often
turns into the world's largest parking lot. I felt relieved not
to face an hour of stop-and-go traffic on the ten-lane Los
Angeles freeway.

My wife, Gaylyn, and I were returning home from an
appointment in Los Angeles. Gentle Christian music
floated through the car as we traveled along.

Suddenly, from the far lane on the other side of the
freeway, a tire catapulted over thirty feet across traffic.
Although traveling at the speed limit of 55 MPH, the cars
were miraculously spaced so that the tire landed in an
empty stretch, then bounced across the remaining lanes.
A tireless Oldsmobile veered onto the shoulder of the

road. Fear danced across my face but immediately evaporated. Endless possibilities for a multi-car accident, but nothing happened.

Near accidents happen to each of us. It's easy to shake these memories off and think about something else. But each incident serves as a reminder of God's protection and daily power. These close calls can be celebrations of God's protection.

Thank you, Lord, for your protection and help daily. Whether I come close to an accident or have a routine day, your hand is always present. Amen.

The Mast
and the Master

Brad Sargent

*The righteous shall thrive like the palm tree; he shall
become mighty like the cedar of Lebanon.*
Psalm 92:12, *MLB*

I'm contemplating getting married and starting a
family. As part of my preparation, I've been on the
lookout for object lessons relating to the concept of the
husband's/father's leadership role. Scripture and life itself
yield many such illustrations. One fascinating analogy I've
found deals with the cedars of Lebanon.

The shipbuilders of old journeyed up into the
mountains of Lebanon in search of the just-right cedar for
two reasons. First, its size, averaging around eighty feet
tall and over a ten-foot diameter. Second, its strength, a
close-grained wood full of resin that prevented dry rot
and insect damage. Usually a mountain-crest grove
produced good candidates.

Did you know, rather than cutting the mast tree immediately, they cut surrounding trees instead? This left the future mast to face the force of the heavy winds alone, thereby becoming much stronger. A number of years later, the shipbuilders harvested their tree and carefully turned it into the main mast to hold their boat's sails.

The obvious analogy compares the adversity of winds and weather to the discipline and suffering that God allows in *our* lives to make *us* strong. Then the Master Shipbuilder places us in the Boat of Life and fills our sails with the winds of the Spirit so we can take our family successfully through Rough Seas to the Land of Promise. Nice parallels.

But what really intrigues me is the thought of this huge, strong mast standing in a boat that floats aimlessly without the right, tiny-in-comparison rudder. Strength is not enough. All the strength and discipline in the world can't make up for lack of proper direction, gained only from the rudder of God's Word.

Well, I've spent my entire fifteen years of adult life on the mountaintop, weathering the storms of singleness, preparing to become a mast. Perhaps we'll know by the turn of the century how well I'm coordinating my masthood with the rudder, and especially with The Master!

My God and Master, help me not to rely on strength alone— even that which has come through adversity you have allowed. Thank you for your precious Word by which I chart and hold true the course for myself and my family. Amen.

You Can't Outgive the Lord!

James C. Dobson

Give, and it will be given to you; good measure,
pressed down, shaken together, running over.
Luke 6:38, *NASB*

My dad was the original soft touch to those who
were hungry. He was an evangelist who journeyed from
place to place to hold revival meetings. Travel was
expensive and we never seemed to have much more
money than was absolutely necessary. One of the
problems was the way churches paid their ministers in
those days. Pastors received a year-round salary but
evangelists were paid only when they worked. Therefore,
my father's income stopped abruptly during
Thanksgiving, Christmas, summer vacation, or any time

he rested. Perhaps that's why we were always near the bottom of the barrel when he was at home. But that didn't stop my father from giving.

I remember Dad going off to speak in a tiny church and coming home ten days later. My mother greeted him warmly and asked how the revival had gone. He was always excited about that subject. Eventually, in moments like this she would get around to asking him about the offering. Women have a way of worrying about things like that.

"How much did they pay you?" she asked.

I can still see my father's face as he smiled and looked at the floor. "Aw..." he stammered. My mother stepped back and looked into his eyes.

"Oh, I get it," she said. "You gave the money away again, didn't you?"

"Myrt," he said, "the pastor there is going through a hard time. His kids are so needy. It just broke my heart. They have holes in their shoes and one of them is going to school on these cold mornings without a coat. I felt I should give the entire fifty dollars to them."

My good mother looked intently at him for a moment and then she smiled. "You know if God told you to do it, it's okay with me."

Then a few days later the inevitable happened. The Dobsons ran completely out of money. There was no reserve to tide us over. That's when my father gathered us in the bedroom for a time of prayer. I remember that day as though it were yesterday. He prayed first.

"Oh Lord, you promised that if we would be faithful with you and your people in our good times, then you would not foget us in our time of need. We have tried to be generous with what you have given us, and now we are calling on you for help."

A very impressionable ten-year-old boy named Jimmy was watching and listening very carefully that day. *What would happen?* he wondered. *Did God hear Dad's prayer?*

The next day an unexpected check for $1200 came for us in the mail. Honestly! That's the way it happened, not just this once but many times. I saw the Lord match my dad's giving stride for stride. No, God never made us wealthy, but my young faith grew by leaps and bounds. I learned that you cannot *outgive* God!

Dear God, thank you for teaching me so many years ago your lesson in giving. And your Word is as true today as it was when it was written. "Give, and it will be given." Amen.

Adapted from the book *Love For A Lifetime* by Dr. James C. Dobson, copyright 1987 by James C. Dobson. Published by Multnomah Press, Portland, Oregon 97266. Used by permission.

The Resurrection Factor

John R. Strubhar

Jesus said...'I am the resurrection and the life."
John 11:25, *NASB*

Though I hate to admit it, worry gets the best of me
from time to time. In fact, I've discovered that worry is one
of life's greatest joy stealers. Indeed, worry is interest paid
on trouble before it comes due. I love Vance Havner's
description: "Worry is like a rocking chair; it will give you
something to do, but it won't get you anywhere!" Robert
Frost once mused, "The reason why worry kills more
people than work is that more people worry than work!"

Nearly two thousand years ago a group of defeated,
despondent, and downcast women got up early in the
morning to go to our Lord's tomb and anoint His body
with spices. As they journeyed toward the tomb, all they
could think of was the Crucifixion, which they had just
witnessed, and the closing of the tomb with the huge
rock. Their hearts were heavy, and worry began its work

in their lives. "Who will roll away the [great] stone for us?" (Mark 16:3). The more they conversed, the greater their anxiety became.

I'm sure Mary Magdelene or some of the women must have thought, "Why go on...this is a wasted trip... we won't be able to get in!" The thought of resurrection had never entered their minds. They were simply performing a routine duty, and the removal of the stone was uppermost in their thinking.

But when they arrived at the tomb they looked up. In doing so, they received the shock of their lives. The obstacle, which they felt was so formidable and impossible for them to remove, was rolled away. They had wasted words and energies on an imagined impossibility!

I must admit, I've found myself from time to time in the shoes of those frenzied, harried, and anxious women. I, too, have a tendency to imagine all the great difficulties before me. I squander precious time by fretting over circumstances beyond me or those I cannot change.

But, like Mary Magdalene, Mary, and Salome, I've discovered that the things I worry about, when I actually encounter them, are not as big or as difficult as I had imagined them to be. When I look up, and take my eyes off myself, my problems, my inadequacies, and the impossibilities in my life, I catch a fresh glimpse of the resurrected Christ. He is alive. The stone is rolled away!

Dear Lord, please forgive me for the hours wasted in useless worry and anxious care. May my focus be upon your adequacy for every issue and concern in my life, because you are alive! Amen.

Identified with Christ

Grayson F. Wyly

Yield yourselves unto God...your members as
instruments of righteousness unto God.
Romans 6:13, *KJV*

A huge white Samoyed dog named Cloud lives at
our house. Except for his big brown eyes and black nose,
every bit of him is white — even his eyelashes.
Neighborhood children love to stop and pet his broad,
furry, "bear" head with the big ruff, and feel his soft ears.
Our home is known as "the house with the big white
dog." We are identified with Cloud.

Our Lord Jesus Christ first identified Himself with us by
being born as a babe in Bethlehem. He did not
immediately appear upon this scene as a man, but rather
yielded Himself as a child to the care of His parents. He
did not upstage the elders of the synagogue. Rather His
discussions with them were polite, yet astonishing to

those who heard Him. Such condescension of God becoming man is truly beyond our comprehension.

Later, as a man, He went about doing good, healing many by the touch of His hands. His compassion was readily showered on those who were helpless and in need of His mercy. His actions toward them caused people to pay attention to His words. He did not tolerate hypocrisy, but condemned it.

Finally, our Lord paid the ultimate penalty. He died for all our sins. Both His hands — hands which had done so much good — were nailed to a rugged cross. He voluntarily died in our place. Identified with us? Yes, completely.

How well do we show our identification with Him? Do our neighbors and fellow workers know we belong to Him?

And what about our hands? Are both yielded to Him, or is one yielded to God while the other is going its own way? Or are we too much like the rich young ruler who did not want to yield the hold his riches had on him, even though the Lord loved him?

Instead, may we yield our hands, as a praise to His saving grace, thus showing to all that we do indeed belong to Christ.

Father, make my yielding to your Spirit more of a reality day by day. May those who know me identify me with your son Jesus Christ. Amen.

Real Men

Harold J. Sala

*And I searched for a man among them who
should...stand in the gap before Me for the land,
that I should not destroy it; but I found no one.*
Ezekiel 22:30, *NASB*

What is a real man, anyway? Especially, a real man,
as God looks at him, because God's perspective is a great
deal different from the media hype and the flamboyant
perspective of our day. The prophet Ezekiel, writing at
least twenty-five hundred years ago, said that God
searched then, too, for a real man.

A real man is authentic and genuine. He never
hesitates to stand alone. A real man has the fortitude to do
right no matter the cost. A real man is not tainted by the
philosophy that "might makes right," or that it's all right to
do something as long as nobody gets hurt.

There are times when a real man is afraid. Even the
celebrated writer Ernest Hemingway defined courage as
"fear that has prayed." A real man would be a fool to fear

no danger, but when he confronts it, he stands his ground without bravado or effrontery.

A real man knows who he is and is secure in himself; he does not need liquor to screw up his courage to face another day. A real man is strong, but his strength is under control.

A real man is never too macho to lead his family in prayer, to be in church, and to acknowledge that the greatest Real Man who ever lived was Jesus Christ, who alone faced the supreme test of death and triumphed over it. A real man is never ashamed to walk in Christ's footsteps and to identify with His cause.

A real man? Chances are he will go unnoticed by the press or the television crews, but be sure, God takes note of real men!

Oh, God, I want to be a real man, free of the pressure to be like everyone else, free to be what you want me to be, and, thus, free to be myself and nothing more. Help me to resist the hype of people around me, rather conform me to the image of your Son. Amen.

Part of God's Family

Jonathan Kattenhorn

*My grace is sufficient for you, for my power is made
perfect in weakness.* 2 Corinthians 12:9, *NIV*

I am a person with cerebral palsy, which means my
muscles do not function well. If I were to walk up to you,
you might think I was going to fall; or when I talk, you
might not understand me. I enjoy making new
acquaintances, learning about people's interests, and
talking with them about the Lord. Just because I have
difficulty communicating does not mean I do not
understand others.

We all have handicaps, but we should do what we can
and not give up. Moses was handicapped in such a way
that it was difficult for him to talk to people. "O Lord,"
Moses said, "I have never been eloquent, neither in the
past nor since you have spoken to your servant. I am slow
of speech and tongue." Then God said to him, "Who gave

116

man his mouth? Who makes him deaf or dumb? Who gives him sight or makes him blind? Is it not I, the Lord?" (Exodus 4:11-12).

And then there's the Apostle Paul who could have said, "I'm handicapped," and given up. But he didn't. He asked the Lord three times to heal him. The Lord told him, "My grace is sufficient for you, my power is made perfect in weakness."

The Lord gave Paul the strength to live with his handicap. Whatever his handicap was, God was able to use him. For Paul went all over Asia telling people about the good news of Jesus Christ and starting several churches.

Once while I was studying my Bible, the Lord helped me to understand John chapter 9, which tells about the blind man. The disciples asked, "Why was this man born blind? Who sinned, this man or his parents?" (verse 2). Jesus explained that no one had sinned, but that this man was born blind that God might be glorified in him. This told me that God wanted to use my handicap for His glory.

The most important thing for each of us is to know Jesus Christ personally as our Savior and Lord. Equally important is to never question why God made us the way we are. I am handicapped in many different ways, but God has given me several opportunties to be an encouragement to other handicapped people.

I became a Christian when I was six years old. When I was eight, I dedicated my life to Christ. When I was thirteen, my Sunday School teacher asked me, "Jon, what do you want to be when you grow up?" I said to her, "I would like to be a director of a Christian camp for the handicapped." The Lord has allowed me to work at a Christian camp for the handicapped for many years.

117

God made me the way I am. The question is not why, but rather, how can I be used in God's family?

Father, thank you for making me part of your family. And thank you for your grace, which is sufficient for all things. Amen.

Is Prayer Gossip?

Larry E. Clark

Come and pray to me, and I will listen.
Jeremiah 29:12, *NIV*

The girl scribbled a tongue-in-cheek message on the blackboard and dashed out of the conference room. The words amused me, yet they reflected some wrong thinking on the part of the missionary kid who wrote them: "In our mission everyone knows everything about everybody else. Some people call this gossip, but we call it prayer requests."

I was in Mexico at the time and often I met with fellow missionaries for prayer. But those words scribbled on the blackboard troubled me. Just a harmless prank? Or did that youngster really feel that prayer was gossip?

Since then I've been examining my prayer life. Often in our meetings I hear that someone has had an accident, is sick, is suffering a rocky marriage. But instead of praying, I let my curious mind swirl in muddy currents where it doesn't belong. Why is he sick? He should have been more careful. Why did their marriage go wrong?

119

God always taps my conscience when I stray from real prayer. I don't have to know all the details.

Our Father invites me to pray to Him and He loves to listen to me. What more can I ask?

Dear Father, help me to call on you more. You know all about my needs. Amen.

Sometimes
the Truth Hurts

Charles R. Swindoll

*Make me know Thy ways, O Lord; teach me Thy
paths. Lead me in Thy truth and teach me, for Thou
art the God of my salvation.*
Psalm 25:4-5, *NASB*

I had a two-and-a-half hour layover at the Denver
airport last winter that proved to be an experience I'll
never forget. I aged about ten years. It wasn't because of
the delay, even though I usually hate to wait. It wasn't
because of incompetent airline personnel. They were
great. It was a small child — simply a preschooler —
who also had to wait with her mother. But this child was
not your basic little girl. She was uncontrollable. Her
mother? You guessed it. Your typical, preoccupied, can't-
be-bothered type...who bargains, threatens, gives in,

wrings her hands, looks away, sighs, *everything but disciplines* her monster...er, *daughter.*

This child did it all. Dumped over ashtrays (I counted four), crawled over every seat (unoccupied or occupied) at least twice, screamed for something to drink or eat until she finally got both several times. The creature grabbed newspapers out of men's hands as they were reading, and finally she did the unpardonable. *She walked all over my shoes.* Now, dear hearts and gentle people, I don't have many untouchables. Having raised four busy children, having been engaged in public service for twenty years, and having been married almost twenty-seven years, I don't have many things left to call strictly my own. But my shoes have withstood the test of time. They are very carefully spit-shined (don't ask why, just accept it), placed in shoe trees each night, protected in the closet when I'm home, and covered with socks when I put them in luggage for travel. As each of my kids (and wife) will tell you, when I'm wearing my shoes, only one person walks on them, and that's me. If someone else steps on them, I have an immediate reaction. And it is not to pray for them. Or smile and say, "That's okay." Or brush the shoe across the back of my other leg and think, "I'll touch it up later." No — my instant reaction is to punch their lights out. I'm just being honest.

Well, I had a slight problem in the Denver airport, you see. The one who stepped onto the holy of holies was a little child. Just a little girl. I rather doubt that she will do that again. I am happy to report she has fully recovered. (Just kidding.) No, I never placed a hand on her. Or a foot! With incredible and rare restraint I bit my tongue and tried to stay out of her path. Finally, when none of us could stand it any longer, the mother was given some loud and directive counsel. And guess what. She was offended.

Why, the very idea that someone would even *think* of her child as being out of control! She was defensive when confronted with the truth. Even though surrounded by sand and ashes from dumped-over ashtrays, litter from several junk food and drink containers, irritated businessmen and women, plus one enraged minister with scuffed shoes, that mother could not imagine how rude we could be when one of us (!) finally and firmly stated, "Get control of your child!"

Father, it is not always easy to hear the truth. At times, we become hurt — and oftentimes defensive. But truth is like medicine and sometimes we have to take it! At times, we're even asked to give it! Help us in those times, dear Lord, to be open to your truth and open to your ways. Amen.

Roasts on a Hamburger Budget

Leonard W. DeWitt

*But my God shall supply all your need according
to his riches in glory by Christ Jesus.*
Philippians 4:19 *KJV*

Does God take a personal interest in the food on
our tables? It would appear from what the Apostle Paul
says that God is open to responding to any legitimate
request made by his children.

Years ago, my wife and I attended a conference for
pastors and their wives. I learned that to attend such
functions can prove to be very costly. When I asked my
wife what her speaker had shared, I discovered that she
had gleaned some very practical ideas.

One idea was a way Sundays could be less hectic for
the first lady of the parsonage. Frequently, by the time we
got home from church and my wife fixed dinner and then
we cleaned up, it was mid-afternoon. The creative idea

was to put a roast (and vegetables) in the oven every Sunday before going to church. Then by the time we got home, dinner would be ready and we'd have saved at least an hour.

Now, doesn't that sound like a great idea? The problem, however, was how were we going to put a roast in the oven each Sunday when our hamburger budget was already overtaxed? I could picture how this concept would make it much easier for my busy wife, so we talked it over as a family and decided to ask God for roasts.

One evening several weeks later the phone rang; it was one of the men from our church asking if I liked beef liver. Since they had just butchered, he asked me to come out early the next morning to pick some up. When I arrived at the farm, I was stunned when the man informed me that he was not only giving me the liver but also a front quarter of that beef!

When I got back to town, I went to my butcher friend to see what he could do with a front quarter. He told me: "Pastor, that is great for roasts and hamburger."

Can you imagine that? Well, why wouldn't God, who gave His people water, manna, and meat in the wilderness, be interested in giving our family roasts to be enjoyed in Washington state?

Peter has some great counsel for us when he says, "Casting all your care upon Him; for He careth for you" (1 Peter 5:7).

Heavenly Father, thank you for your love and for your promise to supply our every need according to your riches. Amen.

Prayer, Not Despair

Tom Carter

*Before they call, I will answer; and while they are
still speaking, I will hear.* Isaiah 65:24, *NASB*

"My son is going to sue you!"

The threatened lawsuit came because I had reported
this man's son to the police for abusing his daughter.
Once I learned of this young father's action, I had no
choice. But the man's final words left me visibly
trembling: "My son will get you for breach of
confidentiality in pastoral counseling!"

After he left, I knelt down and pleaded for God's
protection. My prayer concluded with this request: "O
Lord, please be my mighty fortress." I don't know why I
used those words; they just came to me. Then I

126

remembered that Martin Luther's hymn, "A Mighty Fortress," was based on Psalm 46. So I opened to that passage and began reading. In verses 9 and 10, I came across these words:

> He makes wars to cease to the end of the earth;
> He breaks the bow and cuts the spear in two;
> He burns the chariots with fire.
> Cease striving and know that I am God.

That promise soothed me like a numbing agent rubbed on a baby's teething gums. All at once I was convinced that God would protect me! He would make this personal war cease. He could cut in two the spear that was pointed against me. I stopped trembling, thanked the Lord for His answer to my prayer, and experienced immediate deliverance from worry.

That was several years ago, and I haven't heard from that man or his son since. No lawsuit was filed against me. God not only heard me while I was praying, He answered before I called for help!

What an encouragement to trust Him more.

Father, forgive my lack of prayer in the light of your answers all around me, and my lack of faith in the light of your promises in the Word. Give me grace to trust you more. Amen.

A Conversation with God

Charles R. Brown

Be joyful always; pray continually; give thanks in all circumstances, for this is God's will for you in Christ Jesus. 1 Thessalonians 5:16-17, *NIV*

Lately, Father, my prayer life smells of neglect.
It ought not be like this.
Forgive me, Lord.
Thank you!
I love you, God.

I know I miss so much when I pass by your communion door.
And there is no excuse, for I have never found

that door to be locked.
Usually it is slightly open.
Access is easy.
Yet I deny myself and many others your blessing
as I hurry into another busy day.

Help me, Father of my heart, to think of you
with those first thoughts when I wake from rest.
Help me to learn to pray as Jesus prayed...
"not my will, but yours."
His soul was overwhelmed with sorrow to the
point of death.
Still He prayed.
His conversation with you was bathed in tears.
Time alone with you was a priority.
He is my example.

Father, these moments are good.
I need them so.
I need you so much more!
May I not allow the corrosion of hectic
schedules to separate us.

God, you are so good!
I need you every moment, every hour.
Your presence, just now, is priceless.
Forgive me for the times I have exchanged it
for a few coins.

Oh, great and wonderful God,
thank you for reminding me.
Thank you for keeping me on track;
for helping me take time to focus.
It is a joy to look deeply into the face

of Christ, and fellowship with you.

Thank you. It is good to be here!

Father in heaven, help me to grow strong as a man of prayer. Tap me on the heart often, Lord, to remind me that you are ready to talk. Amen.

A Hungry and Thirsty World

W. James Russell

*If you abide in My word....you shall know the
truth, and the truth shall make you free.*
John 8:31-32, *NKJV*

What are the deep unspoken needs and concerns
in your life? In the lives of those you love? Your family?
Your friends?

In a recent speech, George Gallup, Jr., said, "There is
solid evidence of two powerful undercurrents in our
society: an intensified search for meaning in life, and an
intensified search for meaningful relationships, arising out
of loneliness."

Widespread longing for meaning in life tells us only a
few are at peace with their answers to life's three critical
questions: Where did I come from? Why am I here? Where
am I going?

Intensified search for meaningful relationships means

131

the apostles of moral relativism have failed. It means the values of the "Me" generation and the "Yuppie" culture have failed. Demise of the credibility of philosophies of selfishness is nearly complete. Sadly, the resulting tragedy of millions of broken lives will continue for years to come. Cynical skepticism will continue to be the hallmark of the biblically illiterate.

But truth has a solid ring. It speaks to our inner being and appeals to our yearning for life in a higher dimension. The biblical response to these questions is heard echoing down the corridors of time in the power of this eternal promise: "If you abide in My word....you shall know the truth, and the truth shall make you free."

Who can deny that the highest form of meaningful relationships will be characterized by love, joy, peace, patience, kindness, goodness, gentleness, faithfulness, and self-control? These are spiritual attributes of character established in biblical truth!

Possession, understanding, and application of biblical truth will provide everlasting fulfillment for those searching for meaning in life, and for those searching for meaningful relationships arising out of loneliness.

To be transformed, one must read the Bible faithfully in humble earnestness with an honest, open, and searching mind. Those who hunger and thirst after righteousness will be filled!

Oh, Lord, give me a heart that faithfully and humbly seeks after the truths contained in your Word. And thank you for promising to fill my every need. Amen.

Then June Came

Lawrence A. Tucker

*I tell you that if two of you on earth agree about
anything you ask for, it will be done for you by my
Father in heaven.* Matthew 18:19, *NIV*

There is no sensation like it anywhere. Answered prayer!

From my student pastorate comes a challenging memory. Young, eager, we planned an eight-day youth revival. Seminary classmate, Torrey Johnson, later to found Youth For Christ, was to preach. How our youth prepared! Plans were perfected, personal lives put in order, visits made. But mostly we prayed.

Our prayer list was not general but specific. One by one the names were added until there were eighteen. As a group we claimed the promise that "if two of you shall agree...it shall be done." One by one we claimed those eighteen young people for Christ, in prayer.

Each morning the prayer circle met, then witnessed. When the last day came, every person named had met the Master in an open confession of faith except one, June.

So much in June's life was going against her coming to a saving knowledge of Jesus Christ. Only this was going for her: the effectual, fervent prayers of friends who coveted her, her talent, her beauty for Christ. That last night she was present and surrendered to His great call. God answered prayer.

We sought eighteen, no more, no less. God gave the exact fruit of our seeking. Who can forget His hand in that week's experiences? Now, many years from that exhilirating fulfillment of God's promise, dare I claim it again for a friend, a loved one, a business associate, someone I want to become a child of His grace? Yes, I will! Join me, won't you?

Lord, lay someone's soul upon my heart today, and let me be your instrument for his peace and salvation. Amen.

The Secure Path of Integrity

Edward L. Hayes

The man of integrity walks securely, but he who
takes crooked paths will be found out.
Proverbs 10:9, *NIV*

Integrity is one of the marks of Christian maturity. The
noblest possible ideal in life is to live lives worthy of God
who calls us into His kingdom. Jesus is our example. "He
never sinned, never told a lie (1 Peter 2:22, *TLB*).

Before I dismiss this verse as lofty and unattainable, I
must ask myself: Why is it in the Bible?

The integrity of our faith hinges on the integrity of the
Author and Finisher of our faith. Our own actions of
truthfulness, honesty, and personal integrity must in turn
follow. These two simple facts flow from foundational
principles found in the Bible. *Like leader, like follower* is
good advice.

Do we deplore the immorality of public figures while

135

overlooking promises we have made to our children or mates? What about the white lies we tell, the subtle cover-ups of mistakes to make us look good to others? Or what is our reaction to the mockery we make of the marriage vows when divorce negates "to love and to cherish, till death do us part"?

We can argue smugly that Christianity has a higher ethic than other world religions, while living the lie by actions which reflect an unrepentant spirit. Our arrogance as professing Christians is counter to the humility Christ requires.

Meister Eckhart once observed that "in silence man can most readily preserve his integrity." It is true that our talk betrays our walk. But wouldn't it make more sense to display integrity in actions as well as in silence?

The truth is we live in a real world where no one has a corner on integrity. Saint and sinner alike reflect the fallen nature of our humanity. Those, however, who have the inner light of divine truth and who have the new life in Christ have the capacity to overcome. In short, integrity is now a real possibility because of the power of the Holy Spirit to change our character. "If anyone is in Christ, he is a new creation; the old has gone, the new has come!" (2 Corinthians 5:17, *NIV*).

Lord, I want to walk the secure path of integrity. Keep me from crooked ways which can only destroy my life and witness. Amen.

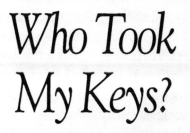

Who Took My Keys?

Stephen F. Holbrook

Whoever wants to become great among you must be your servant, and whoever wants to be first must be your slave — just as the Son of Man did not come to be served, but to serve, and to give his life as a ransom for many. Matthew 20:26-28, *NIV*

When my kids really want to get to me, they do one of the most aggravating things! They take my keys. That's right, my keys.

Now, I've talked with a lot of men about this. And the issue here is control. For a man, it's important to be in control — and to stay in control. Keys symbolize control. The home, the office, the car — everything stays locked until "the man" appears, with his keys.

I remember one evening when I waited with the CEO of a major company outside the front door of his large business. We tried to arouse a janitor to let us in.

Meanwhile, this titan of American business was reduced to a swearing, yelling, out-of-control screamer because he had lost control over entry through that door. When the janitor finally came, he didn't recognize the man and wouldn't let either of us in. Needless to say, the evening was ruined for that CEO.

Control to a man equates to his level of achievement — his greatness, you might say. But in Scripture, our car keys and house keys have little to do with greatness. Rather, God says in the gospel of Matthew, to be great is to be a servant. You want to be chief, be a slave. The pattern is set. God tells us how He did it. We are to follow His lead. And the higher we rise, the more power and control we have, the more we're expected to be the servant of many.

God wants the keys to my life. He wants to be in control. To get serious about my faith means letting God have control, giving up my right to be in charge, and telling Him He's the boss. That's hard for a man to do. Hard, but not impossible.

The next time you're asked to drive the kids in a carpool, help clean up after dinner, or vacuum the carpet, and the feeling of "Hey, do you know who I am?" wells up inside you, remember: *To serve is to be great.*

Lord, I hate giving up control, but I'm deciding to do it right now. I want you to be my Lord. I'm giving you control of my life. Use me in your kingdom. Show me how I can serve others in the family of God. Amen.

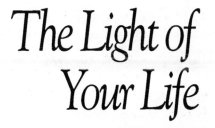

The Light of Your Life

Don M. Aycock

I have come into the world as a light, so that no one who believes in me should stay in darkness.
John 12:46, *NIV*

The threads of habit can become like a steel cable. Lon Chaney, Sr., who starred in the film classic, *The Hunchback of Notre Dame,* said that he had to strap himself into a harness and tie himself hunched over in order to look like a genuine hunchback. But as the days of filming stretched into weeks, Chaney found that the longer he stayed in the stooped-over position, the longer it took him to stand up straight after the day's filming. His body was getting used to being bent over.

This can happen morally, too. A man can choose to stay bent over and misshapen morally rather than to stand up straight in Christ. Rather than live like a human being created in the image of God, he can choose to live in darkness. And when one continually chooses darkness, sooner or later he will lose the ability to see the light.

But we don't have to live in darkness. In fact, we are made for the light. God gave us eyes with which to perceive. More importantly, He gave us a mind and a heart to respond to the light which comes our way in Christ, the light which is truth.

On several occasions my wife and I have visited Mammoth Cave in Kentucky. Twice we have gone into the largest cavern, several hundred feet underground. The guide points out the extensive system of electric lights in the cave, and then, after a warning, shuts them off.

The blackness is so thick and total, it is disorienting. It is darkness so complete you can't see your hand in front of your face. After a few seconds of this complete blackout, the guide lights one match — one tiny match — which illuminates every face in the cavern.

On those occasions I have remembered what the Apostle said about Jesus at the beginning of the gospel of John: "The light shines in the darkness, and the darkness has not overcome it" (1:4, RSV).

The *light* is all around. Will you choose to remain in the dark, or will you choose the light?

Thank you, Father, for the light found in Christ. Help me to live in it always. Amen.

Step Out!

Ray Ortlund

"Lord, if it's you," Peter replied, "tell me to come to you on the water." "Come," he said. Then Peter got down out of the boat and walked on the water to Jesus. Matthew 14:28-29, *NIV*

P eter didn't walk on the water; he walked on the word of Christ. Peter could have walked on anything! Water can't hold a man up, but God's word can hold you on top anywhere.

You've heard about the one who said, "If Jesus tells me to jump through a wall, then it's up to me to jump; and it's up to Him to make a hole in the wall!"

Always remember that when you came to Christ, you became His responsibility. Your part is explicit obedience to everything He tells you to do. His part is covering all the consequences that result from your obedience.

What enormous opportunity is in front of you? Is your life important enough, challenging enough, because you're living on the word of God to you? There's nothing so boring as living a life of total predictability — just doing what you've done for years, and what you know you can do without much effort.

Maybe you're interpreting this in the light of business. An "enormous opportunity" in business may indeed be lying in front of you, and you need to ascertain the promises of God and then step out in faith on His word. In one sense, at least in this phase of your career, that could make your life "important enough, challenging enough."

But how are you doing in living for eternity? Are you shaping all your life in the light of that awesome moment when you stand one-on-One before Him and give an account?

Maybe the great opportunity before you is to become the husband that your wife needs, instead of trying to escape. Maybe it's truly fathering your children, in these years before it's too late. Maybe it's answering the call to become an officer in your church. Maybe it's tithing.

God takes ordinary people (like the fisherman Peter) and does His extraordinary work through them, because they're willing to step out on the word of God.

Lord, it's scary, but today I want to stand on your word for my life. I want to step out of the security of my "boat" and walk on water! Amen.

Did God Get Tired?

Al Munger

*And by the seventh day God completed His work
which He had done; and He rested on the seventh
day from all His work which He had done.*
Genesis 2:2, *NASB*

I hated to go home. The hurt and anger in my wife's
eyes made me feel guilty. Like other workaholics, I half-
heartedly vowed (to myself) to stay away from the office
on my day off. But seven days later, I would head for the
church, saying, "I'll be back in forty minutes. I just want to
write some memos to the staff."

Four, maybe six hours later, I would come home to
face a sweet, tolerant, forgiving, disappointed, and,
sometimes, angry spouse. My response was a little-
controlled resentment and a lot of self-justification. *After
all, I'm a pastor, so many people depend on me. Besides,
it's the Lord's work.* That always seemed to justify my
number-one commitment.

I was wrong. Prior to being assigned to His vineyard, I accepted the privilege and responsibility of being a *husband*. God had declared that I was to love my wife like Christ loved the Church and gave Himself up for her. Yet, here I was giving more attention to people in the congregation than I was giving to my wife.

I was also ignoring another basic command from my heavenly Father, to take a weekly day off and rest. God finished the work of creation in six days and rested on the seventh.

Did God get tired? Was He modeling the concept of a rest day for future generations? Maybe you thought your day off was a product of some labor union's arbitration. Not so. No one really knows how long those creation days were, but a day of rest was in the original plan for all of mankind.

This divine prescription for our health and welfare was illustrated again when God's people were about to enter the Promised Land and were instructed to work the land six years and let it rest every seventh year (Leviticus 25:1-4).

Rest day means time with your wife and children. It means putting your feet up, releasing your mind from the urgent and complex demands of your work. See how the Holy Spirit will renew your mind when you take time to converse with the Lord and feed on His Word. New energy, new dreams, and fresh motivation come when we are resting.

If God needed a day off, maybe we do too!

How blessed I am, Father, to have one day each week to rest, to renew my mind and spirit. Help me to use this day as you intended, and may it be a special day for blessing others. Amen.

Never Alone

Glenn W. Hoerr

*The steps of a man are established by the Lord; and
He delights in his way. When he falls, he shall not
be hurled headlong; because the Lord is the One
who holds his hand* Psalm 37:23-24, *NASB*

It was one of the most beautiful and historic places in
central Germany. The *gasthaus* I was staying in was clean
and comfortable, and the people were friendly. It was a
once-in-a-lifetime opportunity.

Why then was I so miserable? I had never felt such
loneliness before, nor have I since. In fact, I felt so lonely I
was convinced that if I went to sleep, I would die.

I had been in Germany for about three weeks, a
civilian working with the Army Chaplaincy to train
soldiers how to study the Bible and lead Bibles studies. It
was for a minimum of six months and there was no
question I was where God wanted me to be. One fateful
day, however, was the culmination of a series of events
that left me paralyzed with loneliness and fear.

I spoke no German, my car had broken down that

afternoon on the autobahn, I was traveling alone, the person I was to meet at the Army base was not there or even expecting me, and the girl I had dated for the past five months was nine thousand miles away. After what seemed like the longest day of my life, I sat in the cozy, white room of the gasthaus, overwhelmed by the loneliness I felt. My mind raced through one scenario after another, each one leaving me feeling a little worse.

After hours of useless wallowing in self-pity, I decided to begin reading through the book of Psalms. That choice of last resort, which should have been first, brought me to Psalm 37. Like a light being turned on in a dark room, I was reminded that I was in no way alone, for the Lord was holding my hand. With that in mind, I allowed myself to believe God was with me, loved me, and understood how I felt. The paralyzing fear lifted, and I slept soundly the rest of the night.

Once I got my mind thinking right thoughts, I effectively handled being alone, without *feeling* lonely. That day is a constant reminder that I never need to be crippled by feelings of loneliness ever again.

Father, let me always recognize your concern for and presence in my life, and believe that nothing can ever shake me, because, indeed, you are holding my hand. Amen.

When a Cold Shower Just Won't Do!

Wes Haystead

Drink water from your own cistern, and fresh water from your own well. Let your fountain be blessed, and rejoice in the wife of your youth. As a loving hind and a graceful doe, let her breasts satisfy you at all times; be exhilarated always with her love. Proverbs 5:15,18-19, *NASB*

There are certain temptations that never bother some people. Relatively few seem to struggle with the temptation to hijack an airliner, rob a liquor store, use illegal drugs, or commit violent crimes. However, everyone has some temptations that seem to badger them all through life. One of the most common and potentially dangerous is sexual temptation. What man does not respond to an attractive woman or harbor fantasies of having an affair?

Few men have found cold showers or exercise effective means of diminishing responsiveness to female beauty. Far more successful is the wisdom of Proverbs, commanding the man to actively take delight — rejoice, be exhilarated — in sexual relations with his own wife. Pleasure and satisfaction within the marriage bed obviously reduce the allure of dalliance.

Just as obviously, many men use lack of marital satisfaction as an excuse for seeking excitement elsewhere. Unfortunately, they miss a key ingredient in the instructions from Proverbs. Proverbs portrays the man as being responsible for his own attitude. The husband is to *choose* to find enjoyment at home, to expect "fresh water" every time he approaches his wife. Sadly, many men allow their sexual relationship to become stale, so there is little anticipation of pleasure on either side.

Clearly, God holds each husband accountable for loving his wife (Ephesians 5:25-31). This command necessarily includes making the sexual — "one flesh" — part of marriage a process of giving pleasure to her. As in all other areas of living, it is the one who honestly seeks to give who ultimately receives. The husband who sets as his goal to bring delight to his wife is the man for whom marital fidelity is a priceless treasure, not a legalistic burden.

Dear God, I rejoice today that you made both man and woman; I praise you for the gift of sexual pleasure and ask for a measure of your love to bind my wife and me together. Amen.

Look Alive!

David H. Hepburn

*So, whatever it takes, I will be one who lives in the
fresh newness of life of those who are alive from
the dead.* Philippians 3:11, *TLB*

Scanning the real estate ads in today's paper, I realize
we are living in one of the highest cost-of-housing
locations in the entire country! And the price of housing
just continues to rise and rise. Someone has observed that
it is as if the "price tags" have been switched, and things
that used to be valuable have lost their importance and
others have become more precious.

The Apostle Paul, in his letter to the Philippians,
discussed this as it relates to our Christian lives. He says
that he chooses to place a high value on the vitality of his
life in Jesus. Paul confesses his understanding that we are
helpless to save ourselves. And that helplessness has
eternal consequences. He continues in chapter 3, verse 8,

"Everything else is worthless when compared to the priceless gain of knowing Christ Jesus my Lord." Value is in the eye of the beholder!

Powerful words: helpless, worthless, priceless. Does it seem unmanly to confess our helplessness? Does it appear degrading to declare my achievements as worthless? Afterall, those achievements represent valuable years of hard work and sacrifice, and the product of this labor has kept this family comfortable and secure.

This is true for most of us. But still we know we are helpless to save ourselves, and as God's grace glows in its pricelessness, our own achievements pale into insignificance.

I remember when I started my career, my first job. I thought, *Whatever it takes to succeed.* After all, that's the work ethic that has built America! Paul implies that when we realize this new life in Christ for the dynamic experience it is, we shift our focus. We can switch off the success mode, and switch on the desire to be faithful, and echo the Apostle's wonder-working words:

"Whatever it takes, I will be one..."

Lord, help me today to take my eyes off the worthless things and place them on the priceless Redeemer. Change my desires to impress and possess to desires for the fulfillment of your purposes in my life today. Amen.

Appropriating the Gift

Michael B. Reynolds

*For the wages of sin is death, but the gift of God
is eternal life in Christ Jesus our Lord.*
Romans 6:23, *NIV*

A few years ago I was eating lunch by myself in a local restaurant. An elderly gentleman I had known for years was sitting nearby. As he was leaving, he stopped by my table and we chatted briefly.

Later, I waited patiently for the waitress to bring my check. I finally asked her for it, and she informed me the elderly gentleman had paid for my lunch along with his own. Everything was all arranged. All I had to do was get up from my chair and leave.

As I walked by the cashier, she smiled at me with a twinkle in her eye and wished me a good day. I sensed she enjoyed being privy to the gift that had been given me.

Situations like this still happen today. One person takes the initiative, sets up the arrangements for a gift or opportunity of benefit to someone else, and in so doing conveys feelings of warmth and appreciation on the human level.

Salvation is also an opportunity arranged by one person for the benefit of another. Christ has made the arrangements. He has paid the bill and handled all the details. It only requires our response of acceptance by faith. And we are forever grateful for such a simple plan — such a wonderful gift!

Dear Lord, thank you for your thoughtfulness, both in the gift of salvation and in the daily blessings you bring my way. Amen.

Senior Partner

Donald L. Evans, Jr.

*Thus says the Lord, your Redeemer, the Holy One of
Israel: "I am the Lord your God, who teaches you to
profit, who leads you in the way you should go."*
Isaiah 48:17, *RSV*

"Don, I need to talk to you."

I looked up from my work and nodded at Dave, the
supervisor. I followed him to his desk and began to get
that sinking feeling that comes over you when something
is wrong.

Dave's tone was accusing. "You haven't got enough
money in the Harris job."

"What do you mean?" I asked. I was sure I had done
everything right. As a new salesman for a large home
improvement company, I had been extra careful with my
figures on this, my second job.

Dave continued. "The pricing sheets for this work are
different from the others you were given. For these jobs,
the sheets only have labor costs — no materials
included."

Great, I thought to myself. Just great.

"Dave, I wasn't told that, and there's nothing on those sheets that says they are labor-only prices." I said the words defensively.

"That's tough," Dave said. "But I won't approve the job until the profit margin is acceptable."

"What am I going to do now, Lord?" I prayed the words, but they contained little hope. Almost immediately an impression came.

"Solve the problem. Trust Me."

"Lord, the only way I can solve the problem is to pay for the material out of my own pocket. I'll have done the job for nothing, and I'll lose money besides!"

Again came the impression.

"Solve the problem. Trust Me."

I paid for the materials, arranged for their delivery, and put the job folder on Dave's desk without further explanation. Two days later, I was called in to see Bill, the unit manager, who is also Dave's boss.

"Don, you did some nice work on the Harris job." Bill continued to speak and handed me a paper. "Here's a voucher to reimburse you for those materials. Oh, and by the way, because of your discovery about those pricing sheets, we're re-doing them all, so it'll be easier for everybody. Thanks for the way you handled it."

Leaving Bill's office, I prayed: "Thanks, Partner."

Heavenly Father, thanks for guidance in my job, and in every area of my life. Amen.

Why Won't You Believe Me?

W. Terry Whalin

"You believe at last!" Jesus answered.
John 16:31, *NIV*

For weeks, my wife, Gaylyn, struggled with our hand-me-down vacuum cleaner. One day we bought a new one — neatly packed into a small box. Returning home, I attacked the instructions and managed to assemble the machine.

During my test run through our apartment, the vacuum performed like a champ. Another problem solved.

A few days later Gaylyn mentioned that the new machine didn't pick up dirt very well. "What do you mean, it doesn't work?" I sputtered. "It's brand new." Without comment, Gaylyn put away the vacuum.

After Gaylyn had vacuumed the apartment for three weeks with difficulty, I tried cleaning our carpets. I could have done better picking up the dirt on my hands and knees. Reaching for my screwdriver, I opened up the compartment that holds the bag. Dirt and dust poured out on the carpet, but the new bag was empty. Then I discovered a manufacturer's defect. The plastic top of the hose was sealed off and couldn't release material into the bag.

Brother, I thought. *Why didn't I believe Gaylyn in the first place?* God must wonder sometimes why I don't believe Him either. Instead of reading His Word, believing it and responding, I stumble through life. Then I discover answers that have been staring me in the face all along.

God, help me to believe you as I try to listen to your voice and read your Word. Amen.

Part of Dad I Hardly Knew

Brad Sargent

*One generation shall extol Thy works to the
following one, and set forth Thy mighty acts.*
Psalm 145:4, *MLB*

Why is it so hard for us men to talk about our faith?
We pulled out our new *Pictionary®* game at
Christmastime and the menfolk took on the women in
a hot game of this pencil-and-paper charades.

Dad's turn came. He picked a card. The expression on
his face told all — this word was difficult to draw. He
thought and thought, then finally was ready.

"Go!" Mom shouted, flipping over the one-minute
timer.

Dad scribbled as fast as could be expected for
someone who'd suffered a severe stroke seven years
earlier. First he scratched out a long, vertical pole. Next

came a shorter, horizontal crossbar.

"Cross! Crucifix!" my brother-in-law, Bill, and I yelled out.

"No," Dad squeaked out with a voice made an octave higher by one stroke-frozen vocal cord. He continued drawing, while sand flowed. A man took shape on the cross.

We started pouring out possibilies. "Crucify...uhh, crucifixion!"

"No."

"Die...Jesus Christ..." Dad kept shaking his head. Time kept slipping away. "Savior?" Frantic!

"No."

"Calvary?"

The bottom of the tiny hourglass was full. "Time's up," my sister, Romae, said.

"Well, what was it? What was the word?"

Dad looked up from his sketch pad. "*Life.* Jesus dying on the cross gave *life.*"

How many times while growing up had I wondered about Dad and his relationship with God? I remember his saying when people probed about his beliefs, "I have my own private religion." Also, I knew his mother read him Bible stories when he was young, but that about exhausted the topic of Dad and spiritual issues. Thankfully, this clear testimony from my father about his faith in Christ relieved my doubts.

Just five weeks later, Dad passed into the Lord's presence. At his memorial service, I closed the eulogy with his "*Pictionary®* testimony" story so that others could know what Dad believed.

Spiritual realities were a part of Dad I hardly knew when I was young. With God's help, I plan to make sure my children hear and see God's working in my life from the time they are born, to born again, to when I go to be with Him and Dad.

Thank you, Father God, that Jesus is life. Help me share this truth openly. Amen.

Me First!

Tony Sbrana

If you really keep the royal law found in Scripture,
"Love your neighbor as yourself," you are doing
right. James 2:8, *NIV*

Probably you've heard the statement: You can't love others until you love yourself. It's a pretty common theme for pop psychologists these days, and, quite frankly, it sounds reasonable. It even sounds sort of scriptural. If you're supposed to love others as yourself, the first step is to love yourself, right? Wrong.

Loving yourself is not a step at all. The Bible assumes you love yourself already. And rightly so, because the kind of love it speaks of is neither soft sentimentalism nor the narcissistic self-absorption that masquerades as love today.

Instead, it is intensely practical. When you're hungry, do you feed yourself? When you're ragged, do you clothe yourself? When you're threatened by the elements, do you shelter yourself? Well, there you have it...you love yourself!

Now, love others in the same way: Feed your neighbor as you feed yourself; clothe your neighbor as you clothe yourself; shelter your neighbor as you shelter yourself. *Care for* your neighbor as yourself. The current condition of your self-esteem is not even an issue.

God has given us a very practical ruler by which to measure and express our love for others. Ourselves. And such love applies, without qualification, to family and foreigner, boss and beggar, friend and stranger, alike.

Dear Lord, keep me from focusing on myself, as I so often tend to do. And whether it means a serious sacrifice or a simple act of kindness, help me to truly love others. Amen.

A Special Kind of Love

Josh McDowell

*A new commandment I give to you, that you love
one another, even as I have loved you, that you also
love one another.* John 13:34, *NASB*

I had a lot of hatred in my life. It wasn't something
outwardly manifested, but there was a kind of inward
grinding. I was ticked off with people, with things, with
issues. Like so many other people, I was insecure. Every
time I met someone different from me, he became a threat
to me.

But I hated one man more than anyone else in the
world. My father. I hated his guts. To me he was the town
alcoholic. If you're from a small town and one of your
parents is an alcoholic, you know what I'm talking about.
Everybody knows. My friends would come to high school
and make jokes about my father being downtown. They
didn't think it bothered me. I was like other people,

laughing on the outside, but let me tell you, I was crying on the inside. I'd go out in the barn and see my mother beaten so badly she couldn't get up, lying in the manure behind the cows. When we had friends over, I would take my father out, tie him up in the barn, and park the car up around the silo. We would tell our friends he'd had to go somewhere. I don't think anyone could have hated anyone more than I hated my father.

After I made my decision for Christ — maybe five months later — a love from God through Jesus Christ entered my life and was so strong it took that hatred and turned it upside down. I was able to look my father squarely in the eyes and say, "Dad, I love you." And I really meant it. After some of the things I'd done, that shook him up.

When I transferred to a private university I was in a serious car accident. My neck in traction, I was taken home. I'll never forget my father coming into my room. He asked me, "Son, how can you love a father like me?" I said, "Dad, six months ago I despised you." Then I shared with him my conclusions about Jesus Christ: "Dad, I let Christ come into my life. I can't explain it completely but as a result of that relationship I've found the capacity to love and accept not only you but other people just the way they are."

Forty-five minutes later one of the greatest thrills of my life occurred. Somebody in my own family, someone who knew me so well I couldn't pull the wool over his eyes, said to me, "Son, if God can do in my life what I've seen him do in yours, then I want to give him the opportunity." Right there my father prayed with me and trusted Christ.

Dear Lord, thank you for coming into my life and

allowing me to love others with your kind of love. Amen.

Beyond Reputation

John R. Strubhar

*A good name is to be more desired than great
riches, favor is better than silver and gold.*
Proverbs 22:1, *NASB*

In the late 1980s, character has taken it on the chin.
Religious leaders, political "movers and shakers," and
Hollywood celebrities have all come up short. It has
caused me to step back from my busy schedule and affirm
anew that there is nothing truly great in a man except
character. Character is not born in a crisis; character
emerges from a crisis. This is what makes genuine
character much more desirable than a good reputation.

Bishop Fulton Sheen, in his book, *Portraits in a
Darkened Forest,* explains, "Man is very much like a barrel
of apples. The apples that are seen on the top are his
reputation, but the apples that are down below represent
his character."

The point is clear. Reputation is external, whereas
character is internal. Reputation is what you make;
character is what makes you. Reputation is what you need

to get a job; character is what you need to keep the job. Reputation is what you do in the light; character, on the other hand, is what you are in the dark. Reputation is built by what your peers think of you; character is established when only God is present and no one else is around. It is entirely possible to have a good reputation and a questionable character, but it is totally impossible to have an authentic character and not have a dynamic reputation.

To put it another way: When wealth is lost, nothing is lost; when health is lost, something is lost; but when character is lost, all is lost.

In order to develop strength of character, we must conscientiously nurture and cultivate the fruit of the spirit described by the Apostle Paul in Galations 5:22-23. The fruit mentioned has to do with our character development. I am convinced that God is far more interested in what we are (character) than in what we do (reputation).

"Love, joy, and peace" have to do with our character in relation to God. "Patience, kindness, and goodness" have to do with our character in relation to others. Finally, "faithfulness, gentleness, and self-control" have to do with our character in relation to ourselves.

It is God's purpose that we evidence to the world a character that excels, one that is totally transparent and thoroughly Christian; a character that has been captured and controlled by God Himself! By itself, a good reputation just will not do.

O Lord, make my life and work today reflect your character. Help me to make the hard choices which will glorify you and strengthen my character. Amen.

Hey, Watch Where You're Going

Grayson F. Wyly

Look up, and lift up your heads; for your redemption draws nigh. Luke 21:28, *KJV*

With his head down over the handlebars, Jerry rounded the corner at full speed with a wide turn. He didn't see the parked car and plowed right into it, head on. Jerry sailed over the hood like he was shot out of a cannon and landed on the windshield. His bike was all bent out of shape — and so was his pride. He wasn't hurt, though, only embarrassed. Jerry quickly learned to look up and watch where he was going.

As a private pilot, I learned to scan the sky for other aircraft and changing weather conditions. On final approach for landing, it was a good procedure to look to

167

the far end of the runway in order to obtain a proper perspective, a wide-angle view, of the plane's attitude with respect to the ground. Looking at the ground directly in front of the plane would provide only a short-sighted, narrow view of the situation.

Our Lord wants each one of us to have a watchful eye, too, as we go through life. He doesn't want us to be distracted by those things that would be obstacles in our path, like materialism, success as the world sees it, or the me-first syndrome so prevalent today. In addition, He wants our understanding to be enlightened, not just what the crowd thinks, which is usually short-sighted and narrow, but with the proper perspective — with His eyes.

"Look up," His Word tells us. "Lift up your heads." God wants us to look to Him. Learn from Him. And as we do, He will give us eyes, like His, so that we can "run with patience the race that is set before us, looking unto Jesus the author and perfecter of our faith" (Hebrews 12:1-2).

Then, and only then, will we able to watch where we're going!

Father, may the knowledge and wisdom in your Word enlighten my understanding so that my experience does not have to be learned the hard way. Amen.

I Ate the Whole Thing!

James L. Snyder

*Know ye not, that to whom ye yield yourselves
servants to obey, his servants ye are to whom ye
obey; whether of sin unto death, or of obedience
unto righteousness?* Romans 6:16, *KJV*

It all started with one small piece of watermelon.
My intention was to cut one small slice and return the
rest to the refrigerator. At the time, I was fully persuaded
that I was in complete control of my appetite. Then the
inevitable happened. That first piece of icy cold
watermelon led to a second, and then a third, and, in no
time at all, I had eaten the whole thing. I couldn't believe
it. It went so fast, and the last piece was just as good as the
first.

Now eating a whole watermelon is not a catastrophe.
But if this kind of thing happens in some spiritual area of
life, the damage can be extensive and at times permanent.

When some habit or sin begins to control your life, you are at the mercy of that appetite. It is no longer you who are making the decisions in your life. Unfortunately, many of us find ourselves in this kind of situation and don't know how to regain control of those areas.

What do you do when, for some reason, you have forfeited control of certain areas of your life? Where can you turn for the kind of help that will set you free again? *Jesus Christ.* He and He alone has the authority to break the hold that appetite has over you.

As we, in faith, turn to Christ and allow Him to have unquestioned authority over our affairs, we will begin to see some amazing results in our lives. Things we can't explain will begin to happen.

Christ has already overcome the appetites that want to take control of our lives and consume us. Call upon Him to bring you victory.

Dear Jesus, I acknowledge that certain appetites control areas of my life. I purpose to surrender these appetites to you and give you permission to deal with them as you see fit. Amen.

God's Message to Sweethearts

Harold J. Sala

*For this cause shall a man leave his father and
mother, and cleave to his wife. What therefore God
hath joined together, let not man put asunder.*
Mark 10:7,9, *KJV*

Have you ever wondered what happens between
the time a couple stands at a marriage altar, with glowing
eyes and burning hearts, and the time they stand before a
judge to ask for a divorce? Sometimes that something that
destroys a marriage falls like a bomb from the sky, but
more often it comes as quietly and stealthily as a
microscopic disease.

Instead of holy wedlock, it becomes unholy deadlock.
There is one thing you can be certain of: It is not God's
plan for two people to spend their lives in disharmony. It
was God who put within the human heart the power of

attraction that draws two people together and unites their lives.

The Bible tells us that God wants man to find happiness, and it tells him how to do it: Keep love alive. Love is not automatically forever. Your love for a companion must be kept alive or else it will wither and die.

Companionship helps keep love alive. A woman once said, "I love my husband, but we are not very good friends." Her words were telling. Actually, they spelled danger. One of our basic human needs is for companionship, and God made provision for that need to be met in marriage.

Remember how you used to spend lingering hours over a soda before you were married? Chances are you had very little money, but the companionship was something else! If you have that kind of companionship, don't lose it. If you've lost it, regain it.

Let your wife know you love her and want to be with her. Say what's on your heart. But most importantly, be her loving companion — her best friend.

Dear Lord, help me to do what's necessary to keep my love for my wife alive. I want to meet her needs; I want to be close to her; I want to be her best friend. Amen.

Useless Anger

Larry E. Clark

*Refrain from anger and turn from wrath; do not
fret — it leads only to evil.* Psalm 37:8, *NIV*

My wife and I were driving to work while my
passengers discussed the latest atrocity in the morning
news. Anger flowed through me as I listened. Suddenly
Nancy cautioned me: "Your foot's getting heavy." I was
racing along, exceeding the speed limit. My anger could
have led me into a disastrous car wreck.

Injustice angers me. The newspaper stabs me with
reports of violence. Earthquake in Armenia, thousands
killed. A plane crash in Scotland, no survivors. The
innocent face of a child looks out from a missing persons
ad: Kidnapped!

I feel helpless in a violent society that leaves behind so
much suffering. Then pleas for help pour into my
mailbox. Runaway teenagers exploited and abused on
Times Square. Victims of drunk drivers. All that angers me!

Webster defines anger as an "impulse to retaliate." But
how can I fight against the wrongs and hurts of society?

My helplessness in the face of wrongs and injustice leaves me feeling frustrated. Life seems cruel with little I can do about it.

But God is showing me something. The wrongs in the world are like my neglected front yard. Overgrown grass and weeds need an aggressive lawn mower. But I can cut only one swath at a time. I must persist and whittle away at the grass, cutting round and round the yard until the lawn is restored to order. Until next week — when it needs cutting again. An endless task.

The Lord doesn't expect me to restore order to the world. That's His job. My anger and frustration only hinder God's work. Instead, I can contribute my offerings to a genuine need. Or I can intercede in prayer for some sore spot on the earth. Or share my faith with someone who needs a witness.

As I cut my swath where God calls me, doing my part, I trust God to cure the ills of the universe.

Lord, show me how useless my anger is. Help me to be part of your plan to help those in need. Amen.

Remember, God's in Charge

Leonard W. DeWitt

*Therefore, since through God's mercy we have
this ministry, we do not lose heart.*
2 Corinthians 4:1, *NIV*

Are there things happening in your life that are painful and perplexing? Are you wondering why these things are happening and what good could possibly come of these experiences?

Joni Eareckson Tada became a quadriplegic because of a diving accident. What good could possibly come from a beautiful young woman's being so severely injured? Yet, have you considered the ways God has used Joni to touch the world since that time? Her books, art, music, films, and speaking have strengthened and encouraged people the world over.

The Apostle Paul reminded the Corinthians of a very important truth we would all do well to remember: God's

175

in charge. He can take our trials, troubles, and tragedies and transform our lives, thereby, giving us a ministry to others we would never have had in any other way.

We can trust in knowing that God is the God of all strength; He strengthens us in all of our trials and troubles; He strengthens us so that we, in turn, can strengthen others; and, He will enable us to minister to others with the same strength that we received from Him.

Jesus Christ is the Alpha and the Omega, the first and the last, the beginning and the end. Our ability to see ahead is so limited. But our Lord has the whole picture. He has all our lives laid out before Him, and He knows what He wants to accomplish in and through us for His glory and for the good of others.

Dear God, I don't want to be impatient with what's going on around me. Rather, I want to stand still and be amazed at all you will do as I rest in you. Amen.

Something Beautiful of My Life

James E. Bolton

*I will give thanks to Thee, for I am fearfully and
wonderfully made; wonderful are Thy works, and
my soul knows it very well.* Psalm 139:14, *NASB*

As I walk through a forest in autumn, I can see some
of the wonderful works of God. The fiery colors of the
leaves blend together to make a masterpiece of beauty.

While I am praising God for showing me such a
wonderful sight, He gently tells me that He wants to make
my life into something just as beautiful.

"How could that be?" I ask.

"I can put a special beauty of character and an
openness to my ways into your life if you will let me," He
seems to say.

177

I agree to that, even though I don't know all of what I am getting into, except that I know it will be for my ultimate good.

As I am walking back to my car, I stop beside a stream and see my reflection in a pool of water. Then the thought comes to me that just as I can see what I am now, God can see what He wants me to be and what it will take to get me there. Then I realize that God can take the tangled parts of my life and reorganize and fashion them into something He thinks is beautiful. "He sure has a lot of work to do," I sigh.

Just then, a ray of sunlight comes streaming through the trees in front of my path, as if to say that God will be my guiding light. I drive home with this comforting thought.

Thank you, God, for working in my life. Only you can make something beautiful out of the mess I have made. Amen.

Advertise Jesus!

Ray Ortlund

*My tongue will speak of your righteousness and of
your praises all day long.* Psalm 35:28, *NIV*

The *Living Bible* renders the above verse this way: "I
will tell everyone how great and good you are."

The best advertising is a satisfied customer. When a
business gets new customers from satisfied old customers,
they're doing something right. When a doctor gets new
patients from satisfied present patients, he's doing
something right.

And anyone who ever connected himself with Jesus
Christ, through the salvation He offers by His death and
resurrection, becomes a "satisfied customer"! When did
you ever hear anyone say, "Well, I accepted Christ as my
Savior, but He just didn't turn out to be all I thought He
was cracked up to be. To tell you the truth, I'm really
disappointed." No, Christians are often disappointed with
themselves, but they're never disappointed with Jesus!

Then, why aren't we more vocal about Him? Why
don't we tell how He never fails, how He always hears our

prayers, how He's constantly available and close to be our Guide and Comforter and Teacher and Friend?

Remember the story of 2 Kings 7:1-16? Here were five starving lepers who stumbled into an enemy camp and found it totally — and obviously suddenly — abandoned.

> The men who had leprosy reached the edge of the camp and entered one of the tents. They ate and drank, and carried away silver, gold and clothes, and went off and hid them. They returned and entered another tent and took some things from it and hid them also. Then they said to each other, "We're not doing right. This is a day of good news and we are keeping it to ourselves....Let's go at once and report this" (verses 8-9, *NIV*).

And that's the picture of what you find in Christ.

An unbeliever one time asked a Christian, "If I accept your Jesus, what will happen to me?"

The Christian replied, "If you accept my Jesus, you will stumble upon wonder after wonder — and every wonder will be true!"

We dare not hold back. Let's share the riches; there are plenty for all! Let's tell everyone how great and good He is!

Dear God, give me opportunities today to speak of Jesus, and give me your boldness and tact. Amen.

His Way or
My Way?

Stephen F. Holbrook

*Speak to that rock before their eyes and it will pour
out its water....Then Moses raised his arm and
struck the rock twice with his staff. Water
gushed out.* Numbers 20:8,11, *NIV*

Do you know when you have failed at something,
or does someone have to point it out to you? That
probably depends on what you thought what was
expected of you, right?

Well, in the Old Testament book of Numbers, we see
that Moses was a failure in front of the people. But,
interestingly enough, only Moses and God knew about it.
You see, the word went out through the crowd how
Moses had hit that ole rock, and water gushed out! The
people thought this was great stuff. He was their hero.

Now, God had given Moses boundaries. He had said,
"*Speak* to that rock." But Moses didn't do what God

expected of him. No, Moses decided to do God's work in his own way. Instead, Moses struck the rock. And that's when things went awry.

Now, the power of God is in His word. He *spoke* the world and mankind into existence; He *spoke* Lazarus out of the grave; He *spoke* and Satan fled. Yet, how often do we choose to hit, yell, stomp, and kick to get things done, instead of believe God's word for our lives?

I wonder where in my life today I'm doing things my way, figuring just because I'm a child of God He will endorse what I'm doing. After all, look at the stats. The people think I'm great. But what is my standing with God?

Lord God, you set the ocean in its bounds. You have bounds for me, too. Help me to know you and the power of your word in my life, so I will do things your way today and every day. Amen.

A Future Hope

Dan Driver

*There is surely a future hope for you, and your hope
will not be cut off.* Proverbs 23:18, *NIV*

One evening I served as the table topics leader for
my Toastmasters group. Toastmasters is an organization
that works to improve a person's communication and
speaking skills. As table topics leader, I had to give to
members an unknown topic on which they needed to
speak for at least a minute and a half.

The question I asked each of them was, "Imagine you
are a particular person in a certain part of the world, what
would be your expectations for the twenty-first century?"

Each member was given an assigned role. One was an
Argentine cowboy (gaucho), another an African
bushman, another a Filipino fisherman, another an
Eskimo hunter, and finally, a Mexican farmer.

The gaucho expressed concern about whether there
would be enough grass and water for his cattle, and
whether he would be able to make enough money to

keep his family fed, clothed, and sheltered.

The African bushman was concerned about whether there would be enough animals for him to hunt, in order to provide for his family.

The Filipino fisherman worried about pollution and whether there would always be enough fish to go around.

The Eskimo hunter was concerned about the disruption of his way of life from outside forces, which were beyond his control, and whether his traditions could be maintained.

The Mexican farmer was concerned with the fertility of his farm's soil and how the use of pesticides would affect his crops.

What surprised me more than anything else was the lack of hope or optimism from any of these people. I thought there might be some hope expressed about technology providing answers for man's problems, but instead there was overall pessimism. I thought there might be some hope expressed for good will and peace, but there was none.

Listening, I was reminded of the hope which is provided for us in Christ Jesus, and how, despite all that may come, because of my relationship to Him that hope will not be cut off.

Dear God, I thank you for the future hope that's promised in your Word and available to all believers. I'm thankful that hope will never be cut off, but will continue forever, no matter what. Amen.

Love Is
Patient and Kind

Richard Cornelius

*Love is patient, love is kind. It does not envy, it does
not boast, it is not proud.* 1 Corinthians 13:4, *NIV*

W e're all aware of the many marriages that break
up. It's happening to the young. It's happening to the old.
It's happening in the Church and outside the Church.

So, what does it take to hold a marriage together?
When the Bible speaks of love in 1 Corinthians 13 — the
"love chapter" — I believe it refers to a husband and wife.

Many marriages are intact today because love is
patient. When my wife and I go somewhere together,
usually one of us has to wait for the other to finish getting
ready. The one who is ready first waits patiently for the
other.

Love is kind. My wife and I both enjoy doing things for
each other. I enjoy making her coffee in the morning.
Later in the day she enjoys cooking and serving our meals.

185

(She says that's because I always tell her how good they taste.)

We have a caring attitude toward each other and a deep respect for one another. We both enjoy saying "I love you" to one another throughout the day.

We start off each day together with devotions: Scripture and prayer. We look for a Bible verse or biblical concept to think about during the day. We try to make our home a more loving place.

Another thing: Love is eager to believe the best, which truly brings about lasting happiness and joy.

O Lord, give us the spirit of love, which is patience and kindness, toward one another this day. Amen.

A Priceless Gift

Mark McLean

*I am come that they might have life, and that they
might have it more abundantly.* John 10:10, *KJV*

When was the last time you woke up excited to
face a new day — thrilled by the incredible opportunity
of twenty-four more hours on planet Earth? When was the
last time you really enjoyed being alive, not just the
benefits of living or that your life is all that much better
than someone else's, but just that God granted you a new,
fresh start in serving Him?

The Bible says that Christ came to give us abundant
life. If we wake up dreading the new day, we've got to
admit that we're definitely not experiencing all that God
desires for us.

It must amaze God at times to see the hum-drum,
mechanical lives we lead, especially those of us who
claim to follow the most exciting person ever to walk the
earth, the Lord Jesus Christ.

God has granted us a priceless gift in giving us the golden opportunity of a new day, a new chance to glorify Him to those around us.

Now I must admit, there are days I don't wake up overjoyed with the golden opportunity of a new day, because often the same burdens I carried to bed are lying heavy on me again the next morning. But I was not meant to carry those burdens. So I can choose to give them over to the Lord in the same way I chose to pick them up.

A depressed, empty world is looking for some Christians who not only live out Christ's answers in their lives, but who do it joyfully and enthusiastically.

Lord, give me an attitude of gratitude today, if just for the brand-new opportunity to glorify you in my life. Help me to put yesterday's failures behind me and tomorrow's worries in your hands, so that I can concentrate on enjoying today to its fullest. Amen.

Fight to the Finish

Herman D. Rosenberger

*I have fought the good fight, I have finished
the race.* 2 Timothy 4:7, *NKJV*

I had a professor in Bible college who taught New
Testament Greek. His name was Vinton. Vinton loved to
tell of his college days' experiences.

One of his favorite stories had to do with a cross-
country race he entered as a member of his college track
team. The course was a long and grueling one. Many who
started the race did not finish. One by one they dropped
out.

Though Vinton was running far behind the leaders of
the race, he was determined to finish. As the race
progressed, Vinton dropped so far behind he could no
longer see the other contestants. He was running all
alone.

The other runners crossed the finish line with first-,
second-, and third-place winners being recognized.
Thinking that all the contestants had finished the race, the
officials began to leave the area. However, not all the

contestants had completed the race. There was still one more, Vinton. One of the officials, looking over his shoulder to make sure he had left nothing behind, saw a runner coming, barely visible on the horizon. He and the others stopped to see who it was. "Here comes Vinton!" someone shouted, and they all began to cheer. They cheered and cheered, not because Vinton had placed in the race, but because he had persevered and finished.

I have often thought of that story and how it applies to the Christian life. The Apostle Paul saw the Christian life as a race. He had entered that race as a young man and throughout his life he had been true to the prescribed course. The Christian life and ministry had been anything but easy for the Apostle. He had suffered persecution of all sorts, but not once did he think of quitting. Now, as an older Christian who was nearing the end of his earthly life, he was able to say, "I have fought the good fight, I have finished the race."

Lord, give me grace and strength for the race you have set before me. I want to be able to say at my life's end, "I have finshed the race." Amen.

The Thirst Quencher

Tom Carter

If any man is thirsty, let him come to Me and drink.
John 7:37, *NASB*

I felt like I was dying of thirst. And I *was*.

At the age of seventeen, I noticed my body dehydrating for no apparent reason. I couldn't get enough to drink. In desperate attempts to quench my thirst, I would lie on my back in the bathtub and run the cold water into my mouth. I was consuming countless gallons of liquids every day.

But nothing helped. Within a week I had lost twenty-five pounds of water weight. Then my doctor informed me I had diabetes. Smiling, he promised, "A few minutes after I give you this injection, you won't be thirsty anymore."

I laughed in his face.

But he was right! The insulin solved my problem. And

191

for more than twenty-two years I've never missed a scheduled injection — two a day. I know I can't live without it.

Everyone is thirsting for fulfillment. Some try to satisfy their craving in the muddy waters of drugs, illicit relationships, money, work, a particular recreation, or a favorite hobby. But they always return mocked and drier than ever. So do others who assume they can slake their thirst merely by attending church without knowing its Lord.

Jesus possesses the water of life. He alone can meet our heartfelt needs. But many, like me with my physician, laugh in His face.

Dare to trust Him instead!

I heard the voice of Jesus say,
"Behold, I freely give
The living water, thirsty one;
Stoop down and drink and live!"

I came to Jesus and I drank
From that life-giving stream.
My thirst was quenched, my soul revived,
And now I live in Him!

— Horatius Bonar

Lord Jesus, I thirst to know you in a personal way. I can't do without you. I trust you to satisfy this, my deepest need. Amen.

Let's Celebrate

Ray Beeson

*Behold, I bring you good news of a great joy which
shall be for all people; for today in the city of
David there has been born for you a Savior, who
is Christ the Lord.* Luke 2:10-11, *NASB*

Celebration is one of the main themes of the Bible,
especially in the Old Testament where God's people
observed numbers of special occasions. There was the
Passover, the Feast of Unleavened Bread, the Feast of
Tabernacles, special Sabbath days, and many others.

These days were times of observance and remembrance in which much rejoicing took place. They were
not to be solemn and mournful occasions, but rather days
full of joy. The quality of rejoicing with righteousness that
characterized them also set them apart from anything
pagan. They were free from the practice of demonic

rituals, which incorporated fear, lust, and evil worship into other heathen holidays.

Although I like Thanksgiving and Easter more than I do Christmas, as far as holidays are concerned (simply a personal preference), Christmas still marks the day in which hope for humanity entered our world, a day in which light and life penetrated the dark corridors of death and darkness.

Who could not be happy at such an event except the person who is not aware of what really took place that day so many years ago? Who would not celebrate except the person who has been deceived by the darkness? And yet many Christians, some of them well-meaning, have become critical of the occasion, citing materialism as a major objection. Others see the decorated tree as a pagan symbol of worship and therefore criticize the observance, while others proclaim that Santa Claus can really be spelled Satan Claus by simply rearranging a few letters.

I suppose there is really no argument as to what the world has done to most good things in order to extract from them as much monetary gain as possible. And Christmas is no exception.

But wait a minute. Why should we rejoice less over something that is wonderful simply because others only see some selfish advantage in it? Why should we fail to celebrate, with all our hearts, the event that led to our salvation? Why should we withdraw from both giving and receiving? Why should we be negative or bitter or critical because of what the world does to this holiday — especially when God would have us rejoice in the celebration of the birth of Jesus?

No, on the contrary, I refuse to miss a single moment of the wonderful life Jesus brought to me when He came to this planet. I intend to look forward to every Christmas with great anticipation that we will be visited by the very presence of this Christ who now sits at the right hand of the Father.

Excuse me, I hear the sound of pounding; it's my wife, Linda, putting a wreath on the front door, as she readies for our time of celebration. I think I'll go join her.

Heavenly Father, thank you for sending us your son, Jesus. I want to celebrate His coming every day of the year! Amen.

Love Is the Difference

Dave Grant

If you are friendly only to your friends, how are you different from anyone else? Matthew 5:47, *TLB*

T he question has been asked, "If you were arrested for being a Christian, would there be enough evidence to convict you?"

A better question might be, "What have you done this past week that only a child of God would do?" Some of the things that first come to mind, such as praying, worship, reading Scripture, or charity to the needy probably don't qualify, since most people in the world do some of these things at one time or another. For many people their religious rituals and traditions are nothing but a form of subculture.

I think we can find a clue to the answer in the words of Jesus: "It has been said that you should love your

196

friends and hate your enemies, but I say to love your enemies! Bless those who curse you, Do good to those that hate you, Pray for those who persecute you. Only so can you be seen as children of your heavenly Father. If you love only those who love you, what good will it do? If you are friends only to those who are your friends, how are you different from anyone else? Even sinners do that" [Matthew 5:43-47].

This kind of loving doesn't make you a child of God, it *identifies* you as a child of God.

If the difference has something to do with our attitude toward our enemy, it is important to identify who our enemy might be.

An enemy is anyone we consider a threat — someone who could hurt or offend us, someone we feel justified to hate, someone we would like to put out of our life.

Your enemy could be someone who has lived close to you. It could be your [...spouse], or an ex-wife, or a rebellious child, or an in-law, or a business partner.

Our natural inclination is to want to hate or hurt our enemy. The ultimate test of our relationship with the Father, that which identifies us as His child, may be when He asks, "What would you have me do to your enemy?"

The natural response is "Condemn him."

The child of God, the true lover, responds, "Bless him, and give me strength and courage to love him as You do."

To change our world, we will have to do it differently.

Love is the difference!

O Lord, I want to be identified as your child. This day I choose to love others with the kind of love that makes a difference. Amen.

Sincere Love

Robert E. Osman

Love one another earnestly from the heart.
1 Peter 1:22, *RSV*

Mary Martin, the Broadway musical star, was handed a note one evening just before going on stage to perform in *South Pacific*. The note was from Oscar Hammerstein, who was on his deathbed at the time. It said: "Dear Mary, A bell's not a bell until you ring it. A song's not a song until you sing it. Love in your heart is not put there to stay. Love isn't love until you give it away."

Mary acted that night like she had never acted before. Later, when asked about her magnificient performance, she showed the note, and said, "Tonight, I gave my love away."

So often, today, love is confused with charity or friendliness. It has become a loose term, cheapened, degraded, and generally used to suggest sexual desire and not much else.

But the Word, in 1 Peter 1:22, speaks differently of love. Here, it is used to imply that we are not to be hypocritical when we speak of love, but rather we must love earnestly and genuinely. Later in the text, it refers to those who put on the mask of feigned love when associating with others, like an actor who puts on a mask to play the part of another.

Genuine love, sincere love, begins with God. In John 3:16, it says, "God so loved the world, that he gave his only begotten son, that whosoever shall believe in Him will have everlasting life." God's love is a gift.

As men of God we are to sincerely love from the heart. God has given us His love; let us give our love to others.

Lord, help me to reflect your love in my life today and always. Amen.

Leather Jackets

Lawrence A. Tucker

Retain the standard of sound words which you
have heard from me, in the faith and love which
are in Christ Jesus. 2 Timothy 1:13, *NASB*

The church auditorium was warm. As I began my
sermon I noticed the eight-year-old boy in the second
pew. He was wearing a heavy leather jacket, which, in
spite of the warmth, was buttoned all the way to the top.
Not once, before he dozed off, did he unfasten a single
button.

When the service was dismissed, the young fellow
remained to talk. Being curious about the buttoned coat in
such a warm setting, I asked him why he had not taken it
off. "Well, you preach so long I get sleepy, and my coat
holds me up so I don't fall over."

So, that was it. He had learned that when he could not
control the sleep situation his coat would hold him steady.
Isn't that something we all need to learn? When we
become involved in situations which we cannot control,
don't we need something to keep us steady? Something to

offer encouragement to our sense of integrity, our need for a stable character, an outward, or inward, source of strength in some setting of weakness.

Maybe we have come from backgrounds where loose attitudes toward the sacredness of the marriage vows prevailed. Or, where a man's character was measured by his proneness to alcohol or narcotics. Or, maybe to an undisciplined kind of recreation to support life.

I know of a youthful home, on the verge of collapsing, which was held steady by the example of an older couple faithful to their vows. *A leather jacket!* A young minister held steady to his calling by memory of fellow students praying for him. *A leather jacket.*

It would be wonderful if we were all in the business of placing "leather jackets" of influence, teaching, witnessing, praying, and many other kinds of outward support around those within our sphere of example. In so doing, we would help to hold them erect, during the long sermon of experience, until their calling in Christ Jesus is secure.

My Lord and Savior, thank you for those who have been my encouragement, example, and support during times when I might have fallen. Amen.

Panic or Prayer?

Al Munger

*Cast your burden upon the Lord, and He will
sustain you; He will never allow the righteous
to be shaken.* Psalm 55:22, *NASB*

A former Navy frog man, Rick was now a law officer
and my diving buddy. We had taken my sixteen-foot boat
north in Hood Canal, Washington, to Claus Rocks near the
mouth of Mats Mats Bay. After anchoring, we put on our
gear and dropped over the side into a beautiful,
underwater garden of kelp and sea anemones, swimming
scallops, and a school of sea bass.

In the water we were weightless. The only sound was
air escaping from our scuba regulators. Thirty feet above,
we could see the brightness of the sun. We felt good. It
wasn't hard to get close to the fish for accurate spear
shots, and we found a plentiful supply of rock scallops for
our goody bags.

An hour passed quickly. Rick motioned he was going
back to the boat. I wanted more fish, but I sensed my air
was getting low. I decided to stay a little longer. *Just two*

more scallops. Finally I had my limit — my bag was full.

By this time my air tank was empty, so swimming to the boat underwater was out of the question. I surfaced in the kelp bed and discovered the tide had changed. It was now running against me. The boat was not more than two hundred feet away, but I was having a tough time fighting the current and kelp. The heavy bag of fish and scallops drained my strength. I was tired. Too tired. Fear began to drive my arms and legs. Again I checked the boat location. My partner, Rick, was nowhere in sight. The panic bell began to ring. *I can't panic; I've got to keep my head. Oh, God, help me!*

In a moment, I felt Rick's hand on my arm. Without a word he took my bag, began pushing through the kelp, and together we made it back to the boat.

Does your burden ever threaten to pull you under? Have you ever been on the edge of panic? How good it is to call on the Lord, to experience His strength as He takes our burdens and leads us through our crises. The promise is simply, "He will sustain you." And that is enough to get us back to the boat, back to safety.

Thank you, Lord, for the rescue that day, and for so many other times when I am not even aware of it. Forgive me for struggling to do it myself in so many areas of life. Thank you for being ever present to take my burden and lead me out of danger. Amen.

Mixed Blessings

Donald L. Evans, Jr.

*And we know that in all things God works for the
good of those who love him, who have been called
according to his purpose.* Romans 8:28, *NIV*

While enjoying a camping experience recently, the
ranger warned me that bears were raiding the
campground due to a shortage of their natural foods.

"Be sure to lock up your food in your car at night," he
said. "If you leave your ice chest and food box out, the
bears will destroy them."

Sure enough, each night I was there, the bears came,
knocking over trash receptacles to get at the garbage
inside.

After a few nights of this, I learned of one camping
group who did not heed the warning. They left their food
outside, and the bears destroyed the campsite while
enjoying the easy pickings.

"We want our money back!" the group demanded.
"We didn't count on this!"

Apparently these folks would accept the trees,

mountains, and fresh air, but not the bears. God made all these things, however. I thought perhaps that this group might have been better advised to heed the ranger's warning and enjoy this natural area and its native inhabitants as God had prepared it.

Then a question formed in my mind. How many times had I been willing to accept only part of God's plan for me?

I'd said it many times: "Give me the blessings, Lord, but spare me from the challenges and problems."

The fact is that all that God allows me to experience is to my good and to my highest development. The next time I encounter "bears" in my life, let me not run from them, but rather face them head-on (heeding any appropriate warnings), learn from them, and grow.

Holy Father, I thank you for all of life. I affirm your wisdom and control. Keep my eyes constantly on you. Amen.

Realizing His Riches

Glenn W. Hoerr

And my God shall supply all your needs
according to His riches in glory in Christ Jesus.
Philippians 4:19, *NASB*

W e were a comfortably adjusted family of three,
living in a reasonably priced two-bedroom apartment,
when we learned we were to become a family of four.
Not that we minded having a second child, but we
thought the timing could have been a little better. As we
began to realize some of the changes involved, we knew
the months ahead would be trying.

One major change involved housing. We would need
more space. The challenge was formidable because we
lived in an area of tight, expensive housing. My wife and I
sat down and listed what we felt we needed in a new
home, whether we rented or purchased. We had no
money for a down payment and would not qualify for a
loan anyway, but we continued to make our list. Three

bedrooms, two baths, fenced-in yard, family or living room for having people over, ample parking, and close to work were items we felt reasonable to pray for. Also included in our prayers were what we would pay for a rental and what we could afford if we purchased. To make our prayer more specific, we wanted to be in our new place before the baby arrived in early December. That left almost seven months. Our search then began.

Time after time we found a place close to what we had prayed about, but were always too late. Someone else had either just rented or bought it.

As the end of September approached, I got a lead on a possible purchase. I wrote to the owner. Four days later he called and said he believed our interest in his house was an answer to his prayers. He said that the house he was selling had four bedrooms, a family room and a living room, a fenced-in yard, it was a mile from my work, it had plenty of parking, and was in one of the best neighborhoods — and he would carry the loan. Our monthly payment was within one dollar of what we had prayed. We moved in our new home in November, just ten days before our baby was born.

God had not only met our need, He did much more. I learned in a clear and refreshing way that God doesn't give to us out of our need, rather He gives to us out of His riches. Now, whenever I have a need, I find it much easier to trust God with the uncertainty, because I know He will not only meet it, but will go far beyond, by giving out of His riches in glory.

Father, help me to trust you completely with any need I have and to believe you will answer according to your greatness. Amen.

Plow up the Fallow Ground

Dick Hagerman

*Sow for yourselves righteousness, reap the fruit of
unfailing love, and break up your unplowed
ground; for it is time to seek the Lord, until he comes
and showers righteousness on you.*
Hosea 10:12, *NIV*

In Idaho, as in all states, there are two types of
ground: fallow and plowed.

Fallow ground is contented ground. It hasn't been
shocked by an eight-bottom plow or agitated by sectional
disk machinery. It has stability in that it grows
monotonous crops of gray sagebrush and brown
chetegrass. It is safe and undisturbed, and sometimes
rattlesnakes and rabbits use it for a home. It always
remains the same, while the fields around it change from
brown to green and back to brown again. Safe and
undisturbed, fallow ground is the picture of contentment.

But it pays a price for its serenity. Fallow ground never witnesses the miracle of new life, nor can it bear fruit, because it is not prepared to accept the seeds that produce a crop.

Plowed ground is the opposite of this stability. There is no contentment in plowed ground. The eight-bottom plow tears it apart and the huge sectional disk pulverizes it to make a bed for new seeds. The field has changed. The plow and disk have chased away the rattlesnakes and the rabbits. They have grubbed out the sagebrush and chetegrass. Yet, the plowed ground is rewarded for its sacrifice as it produces golden wheat, green-leafed alfalfa, and even-eared corn. God is at work in the plowed field demonstrating new and wondrous examples of His power of creation.

Hosea's comment made me think: *Lives are like land — fallow or plowed.*

A fallow life is content with past accomplishments and the monotonous crop it grows. "To be" takes the place of "to become," and the life no longer lets God plow it up in order to produce a new crop.

A plowed life is not content. It lets the plow of the Bible and the disk of the Holy Spirit pulverize it into fine soil where the seeds of God can be planted and new crops grown.

Lord, plow me to pieces and disk me to soft soil. Then your seeds will fall on soil ready to grow new crops each day. Amen.

Honesty Is Still the Best Policy

Edward L. Hayes

Provide things honest in the sight of all.
Romans 12:17, *KJV*

Honesty is sometimes found in strange places.
Waiting to board a flight to South Africa from New York City, I heard my name being paged. Just a few minutes before, I had called my wife in California to say a second good-bye before the long flight to the Southern Hemisphere.

"Is this your wallet?" the agent asked as I approached the counter.

"Where was it found?" I asked.

"A woman just turned it in. She found it in a phone booth."

Turning quickly to see if I could thank the lady and reward her, I suddenly realized that an honest person had disappeared without thought of reward.

That incident helped shape my own convictions about basic honesty.

Honesty is the best policy, as the saying goes. It works in business as it does in all of life. Without honesty, relationships fail, business turns sour, and self-respect goes right out the door. Honesty is the bedrock upon which we build our marriages, conduct our businesses, and sell our products.

Honesty is a characteristic of the Christian life. In the Bible it appears often like street lights to show us the way to a productive and wholesome life. The word *honesty* appears some one hundred times in the New Testament. No peripheral truth, it is front and center on stage along with authenticity and integrity. Our whole concept of self-respect flows from its pure springs like refreshingly pure water.

Honesty is better than wealth. Wealth often corrupts, but honesty wears well over the long haul and often brings richer rewards than money. A Christian's only wealth must lie in honesty and good works, according to 1 Timothy 6:18.

Scholarship can confuse; learning can bewilder; efficiency can chill; aggressiveness can antagonize; but honesty is attractive. That which tugs and pulls at people's hearts to bring them to Christ is simple honesty.

I once read this list of ten things to remember:
The value of time
The success of perserverance
The pleasure of working
The dignity of simplicity
The worth of character
The power of kindness
The obligation of duty
The influence of example

The wisdom of economy
The witness of patience
I'd like to add an eleventh: *the attractiveness of honesty.*

Lord, help me to be an honest man even when no one is watching. Reshape my character to reflect your own. Amen.

A Father's Journal

Charles R. Brown

*One generation will commend your works to
another; they will tell of your mighty acts.*
Psalm 145:4, *NIV*

Keeping a journal is not as difficult as it might seem.
Yes, it does take time — maybe five or ten minutes a
week. But, you don't have to be a great storyteller or a
master of the language. And spelling isn't all that
important.

Memory lane tends to get a bit cluttered as we make
our way along our roads of life. With a glance through the
pages of our journals we can relive special moments in
our histories.

Entries don't have to be long or elaborate. For
example: "1979 Shonda, as we went through the bank
drive-thru, 'hamburger, fries.'" With this brief line, I can

sketch the entire episode with my two-year-old at that time.

Here's another simple note: "11-28-80: Jon (7) — talking with his older brothers. They had lots of information about coming events and things. 'How come you guys know so much?'"

The pages become documents of praise and worship. I have a few lines dated "Sunday, October 15...Car trouble. Leaky radiator. Called friend...Same day — afternoon. _____ called to tell us of the homegoing of _____ (age 31)...and I have car trouble — but our great God is concerned about both."

Perhaps one day my children will pick up the notebook that has these words written: "Planted plum tree Tuesday, April 12, 1977, on the west side of the house. Dad, Wes, Mike, and Jon prayed for God's life-giving blessing. Grandpa brought it from his tree in Oceanside."

The lines you have written may never be read by anyone else. Or, perhaps, they will be enjoyed by your children and their children and their children. There's no limit to what the Spirit of God might do with your journal for many years to come.

Grant wisdom and direction, Lord, as I make entries in my journal. In the end may you be praised and glorified by all who read. Amen.

Finding Peace in a Turbulent World

Don M. Aycock

Keep putting into practice all you learned from me and saw me doing, and the God of peace will be with you. Philippians 4:9, *TLB*

You may recall the name John Bunyan. He wrote the classic, *Pilgrim's Progress*. This book traces the journey of Pilgrim to the eternal city. At one point Pilgrim is taken into a room described as wonderful and light-filled. The room is called *Peace*.

I'd love to have a room called peace — a sort of hideaway, or, at least, a place to go when life gets too hectic. Maybe you have such a place — a secluded spot on a nearby river, or a special chair in the backyard under a favorite oak tree. But life isn't designed in such a way that we can just run off to our favorite spot whenever we'd like to for a little rest and relaxation.

In his letter to the Philippians, the Apostle Paul

suggests three actions for us to take in order to develop peace on a daily basis. The first is to settle our differences with others. "Quarrel no more — be friends again," Paul says in verse 2. Quarreling between friends had led to unrest in the church. Paul admonished the two who were fighting to work on settling their differences before they could find peace.

Next, Paul says to establish and maintain a permanent prayer life. "Pray about everything," he says in verse 6. "Tell God your needs and don't forget to thank him for his answers," he continues.

And, third, we must keep our minds on higher things. "Fix your thoughts on what is true and good and right. Think about things that are pure and lovely, and dwell on the fine, good things in others. Think about all you can praise God for and be glad about" (verse 8).

We may not have in our house a room called peace. And we will not always be able to run to our favorite spot for some rest and solitude when life gets too hectic. But if we practice the principles set forth by Paul to the Philippians, we can be guaranteed: The God of peace will be with you — and me.

Dear Father, life is so hectic at times. Help me find the inner peace that comes from knowing you and putting into practice the precepts in your Word. Then give me strength and opportunity to share Christ, the Prince of Peace, with others. Amen.

Acquire True Wealth

Ray Ortlund

*My God will meet all your needs according to
his glorious riches in Christ Jesus.*
Philippians 4:19, *NIV*

"Lord, I want to be your man: doctrinally sound,
thoroughly evangelical and respected, and, if you don't
mind, rich."

That's the prayer — consciously or unconsciously —
of most Christian men. We want to follow Jesus,
somewhat, but can't we somehow manage to have the
best of both worlds?

No, we can't. Jesus flat out said it: "You cannot serve
both God and Money" (Matthew 6:24).

If this is a struggle in your own heart, settle it right
now, once and for all.

Jesus, in Luke 12:15-21, told about a fellow who with
great ambition, perseverance and hard work built up a
great nest egg.

Sounds like a winner!

But, "God said to him, 'You fool.'"

And Jesus' comment was, "Be on your guard

against all kinds of greed!" Greed for possessions, greed for status, greed for power and influence. This is the exact opposite of our society's ways and our own natural inclinations. No wonder He says, "Be on your guard!"

Well, then, what's the alternative? Poverty? Not at all.

The alternative is setting your sights on God and going hard after Him — and trusting Him to take care of you. Of course, you'll be conscientious in the way you earn a living (2 Thessalonians 3:11-13). But spend your energies, your ambition, your perseverance, to become the most godly man possible. And God will spend His limitless energies taking care of you and rewarding you! Such a deal.

Queen Victoria one time asked a man to go abroad on an errand for her that would require several months' time.

"Your Majesty," he said, "I beg you to get somebody else; my business would really suffer."

"Sir," said Queen Victoria, drawing herself up to her full height, "if you will take care of my business, I will take care of your business."

When you have put yourself totally in the hands of a loving God, then you're poised in any economic situation. Poverty won't embarrass you, and every need will be supplied. Wealth won't make you feel guilty; this is God's decision.

Mostly, just praise God. Go hard after Him. As your security grows in Him, then you "can do all things" (Philippians 4:13) — handle all situations.

Lord God, give me life priorities that will make me rich in you, rich for eternity. Amen.

How Much Is Too Much?

Lloyd John Ogilvie

*For the people of this world are more shrewd in
dealing with their own kind than are the
people of the light.* Luke 16:8, *NIV*

I had a good visit with one of America's most successful businessmen on a cross-country flight recently. He has
risen from a very humble background to immense wealth.
I asked him the secret of his success. His response was
very interesting.

"Shrewdness!" was his one-word reply.

I was shocked by his frankness.

He went on to say that he spent every waking hour
thinking, scheming, planning, developing and putting
deals together. In it all he has tried to be completely honest in all his affairs!

I couldn't help but admire his single-mindedness. He
knew what he wanted and left nothing to chance. He

worked hard to achieve his goals. All the power of his intellect, the strength of his seemingly limitless energies, the determination of his iron will and the resources of his calculated discernment of people were employed to accomplish his goals.

When it seemed natural and unforced, I shifted our conversation into what the man believed about God. There was a long silence. He admitted that he had not taken any time to think about that. He was astonished by my response: "If you ever put the same time, energy and will into being a disciple of Jesus Christ, you would be a contemporary Apostle Paul."

The man's response was thoughtful and reflective: "Nobody has ever challenged me with that!"

The conversation with my traveling companion made a deep impression on me. It forced me to wonder if I could say that Jesus Christ meant as much to me as this man's career does to him. That led me into a long analysis of people I know in business, entertainment, government and sports who invest uncalculable personal thought and resources to get ahead. No cost is too high; no sacrifice too demanding. Scheming, study, rehearsal, practice and determination are committed as a small price for perfection and success. I often wonder what would happen if Christians took following Jesus Christ as seriously as these people take getting ahead.

Father, help me to focus daily on following you with all my determination and all my resources. Amen.

Adapted from *Autobiography of God* by Lloyd John Ogilvie. Copyright 1979 by Regal Books, a division of Gospel Light Publications, Ventura, CA. Used by permission.

Restored

Herman D. Rosenberger

*Brethren, if a man is overtaken in any trespass, you
who are spiritual restore such a one in a spirit of
gentleness, considering yourself lest you also
be tempted.* Galatians 6:1, *NKJV*

Salvage crews were dispatched from mainland
U.S.A. to the U.S. Naval base at Pearl Harbor, Hawaii,
immediately after the devastating aerial attack by the
Japanese on December 7, 1941. Their mission was to
salvage as many of the sunken U.S. warships as possible.
This would be the first step in the effort to restore the
ships to fitness for battle.

I watched as the brave divers, members of the salvage
crew, boarded the sunken battleship *West Virginia*. They
went below decks and sealed off all of the compartments.
Heavy-duty water pumps were positioned throughout the
great ship, and the emptying process began. Daily I could
see the waterline recede on the hull as the battleship
began to rise out of the water.

Months passed before the *West Virginia* was fully

restored, but restored it was! With a new captain and crew aboard, bristling with new cannons and antiaircraft guns, and the American flag flying from the mast, it was a sight I will never forget. As it sailed out of the harbor to join the fleet to do battle against the enemy, there were shouts and cheers; the great battleship had been restored!

The restoration of the *West Virginia* is somewhat analogous of the restoration of fallen man. By nature, man is a sinner, sunken to the bottom, needing a Savior. God sent His son Jesus from heaven to save us from sin's penalty and power. As we have faith in Him, He comes aboard our vessel, so to speak, and restores us to wholeness. We are then enabled by His Spirit to join in the effort to restore others to wholeness.

Lord, work through me today, and always, to restore others to fellowship with you. Amen.

Speaking from the Shadows

John R. Strubhar

Though he is dead, he still speaks.
Hebrews 11:4, *NASB*

It hit me like gangbusters this past Christmas, amidst all of the festive joy and celebration. An important figure is annually forgotten.

He appears to be an onlooker or even an intruder. He doesn't say much, and, for the most part, remains silent. The limelight bothers him. He's a common man. He is not on a campaign to impress anyone. Painters and sculptors, alike, have ignored him or relegated him to a secondary role in their nativity scenes. Even the nameless shepherds and searching Magi receive more attention than he does. He becomes visible shortly before Christ's birth, is mentioned in the Gospel narratives during our Lord's formative years as a human being, and then recedes from any other notice in the biblical record. He is Joseph, the

224

forgotten man in the stable.

How unfortunate. Surely, he must have been a remarkable man to have been selected by God to be the earthly father of God incarnate! Scripture bears testimony to the great faith and obedience of Joseph. In Matthew 1:20, an angel asks him to believe that his beloved Mary, although with child, has been faithful to only him. Joesph does not question the angel's word but does just as he is commanded, taking Mary to be his wife. Then again, when he is warned in a dream to take Mary and the young child, Jesus, to Egypt, in order to escape King Herod's devilish plot, he obeys immediately without hesitation. Joseph is a God-dependent man! His obedience and faith are extraordinary. They are beyond the level where many of us are living.

As the Christ child grows, Joseph takes the lead in caring, nurturing and even discipling Him. Together with Mary, he presents the young child to God in a formal act of dedication. He doesn't relegate his spiritual responsibilities as a father to his wife. Every year both Joseph and Mary journey to Jerusalem to celebrate the Feast of the Passover. "And the Child continued to grow and become strong, increasing in wisdom; and the grace of God was upon Him" (Luke 2:40).

As a father, Joseph earns the respect of our Lord through his loving, yet firm leadership. In concert, he and Mary orchestrate the kind of home life where obedience is expected and regularly affirmed. All of this is possible because Joseph is a God-devoted man.

The forgotten man in the stable is, in reality, a great giant of the faith. His unique specialness cannot be questioned. May we, as men today, take our fatherly responsibilities as seriously as Joseph did and provide an enriching environment for our families that will mold them into God's special people. The buck stops at our desks, men. The man in the shadows is a worthy role model!

Dear Lord, give me the strength to exercise spiritual leadership in my home. May my first response to you be one of complete and total obedience. May my family grow "in wisdom and stature, and in favor with God and men." Amen.

My First Love

Tom Carter

I have this against you, that you have left your
first love. Revelation 2:4, *NASB*

"You'll have to give up tennis," the doctor announced, rather abruptly. My heart sank.

That morning, I had stumbled on the sidewalk and broken my wrist. I was in my senior year at college and the defending tennis champion in our conference of eight universities. And the season was about to begin.

That afternoon, bitterness set it. "Is this what I get for being a Christian? Lord, why couldn't I have broken my wrist ten weeks later? I have to defend my championship! I can't quit now."

God had a message for me, too. "Tennis has become your life. You love it more than me."

I struggled all that night, clinging to the idol the heavenly Father wanted to tear from me. By morning I was physically — and spiritually — exhausted. "Okay, Lord, I know I'll never be at peace again until I put you first in my life. Take the tennis. It's yours." Those words didn't come easily. But they voiced a sincere commitment.

The next morning, I returned to the doctor so he could inspect my cast, which by now had hardened. "You'll have a little trouble tossing up the tennis ball with this cast on your arm," he remarked.

"What do you mean?" I inquired. "Yesterday you told me I had to quit tennis."

"Well, your right arm is still in good shape. And that's the one you play with, isn't it? If you can manage, go ahead and compete."

I think I felt a little like Abraham, when he had placed his son, Isaac, on the altar of sacrifice, only to have God give him back (Genesis 22). That season, with my left forearm in a cast, I successfully defended my title as conference champion. Then I hung up my rackets for good to prepare myself in seminary for the ministry.

I look back on my tennis career with fond memories. But my true love lies elsewhere.

Dear Jesus, make me aware of the things that daily compete with my devotion for you. I want to love you, not routinely, but sincerely and deeply. Amen.

Night Blindness

David H. Hepburn

*This is the message God has given us to pass on
to you: that God is Light and in him is no
darkness at all.* 1 John 1:5, *TLB*

Light is so attractive, and yet the Apostle John says
some men for petty reasons prefer wandering in spiritual
darkness, and soon the darkness has made them blind so
that they cannot see the way.

The terrible destructive floods of 1980 left our home in
the Santa Cruz Mountains of Northern California without
heat or light for six days and nights. We were literally
powerless! The winter nights were cold and the limited
supply of firewood represented our full potential for
keeping warm. To conserve heat we blanketed off the
living room until we were literally sealed in that space.

Although the novelty of popcorn popped in the
fireplace and roasted hot dogs wore off, we had adjusted.
Each evening found us up close to the fire for a game of
Scrabble.®

Then, one evening, neighbors Tom and Denise called

from the front door. Pulling back the blanket as they stumbled in, they shouted, "Why are you two sitting there in the dark?" Power had been restored two hours earlier, but our now-established routine had isolated us. I guess we had not expected the power to come back on, the lights to shine normally, or the fridge to start humming again!

There have been times in my life when I have felt powerless. Oh, I could still work, fish, ride my motorcycle, even write new songs. But all by routine; not always in the power of His light.

At the end of what once seemed a long time of "power failure," these words were an expression of the resurgence of God's power expressed in my life:

> I came as a pauper, stripped of my pride,
> And knelt at the cross where the Saviour died.
> His grace and forgiveness to me were applied,
> And now I'm a child of the King.

It feels good to have the power restored.

Whenever I feel like my prayer fuse or devotion fuse or ministry fuse is blown, I can always direct my feet to the sunny side of the street. That's where God is — in the light!

Lord, forgive me when I sit in the dark, feeling cut off and powerless. Make this a day full of yourself. Help me to continually walk in your light. Amen.

The True Mark of a Man

Harold J. Sala

*Blessed is the man who walks not in the counsel of
the ungodly, nor stands in the path of sinners, nor
sits in the seat of the scornful: but his delight is in
the law of the Lord, and in His law he meditates
day and night.* Psalm 1:1-2, *NKJV*

What is the true mark of a man? His age, his worth,
his ideas, his accomplishments?

To the Eastern mind, man is often measured by the
length of his beard or the whiteness of his hair. Thus,
wisdom in the Orient is synonymous with age.

To the businessman, worth is often considered to be
the true mark of a man. We say this person or that person
is worth a million dollars. How he made that money is
often not important. So I must conclude that worth is not
necessarily the true mark of a man.

The philosopher would suggest that a man's ideas are

his true mark. Victor Hugo, the French philosopher, recognized this when he said, "Nothing in all the world is as powerful as an idea whose time has come."

The pragmatist would say, "Away with ideas. Show me what a man has done — his accomplishments — and I will show you his true mark."

When Richard Nixon was president, he stood before the bier of Dwight Eisenhower in the U.S. Capitol rotunda and said these words: "We find ourselves today thinking first not of his deeds but of his character. It was the character of the man, not what he did, but what he was." I believe a biblical truth was expressed, for in the sight of God, the true mark of a man is his character — his being — not his accomplishments, his ideas, or his net worth.

God's perspective is certainly different from ours. We put the emphasis on doing; God puts it on being. We put the emphasis on accomplishment; God puts it on character.

Consider this: What you are is far more important than what you will ever do.

Lord, help me remember that what I am as a husband, father, son, and brother will endure long after my accomplishments and titles have been forgotten. Amen.

Red Lights and Prayers

Stephen F. Holbrook

Wait for the Lord; be strong and take heart and wait for the Lord. Psalm 27:14, *NIV*

If you're a typical man, you don't use those hand dryers — blowers, really — that have replaced paper towels in public bathrooms. You wipe your hands on your pants or wave them in the air, but you are not going to wait and rub, rub, rub under a dryer. You have more important things to do, right?

Psalm 27 tells me to be comfortable waiting. This is unnatural. I'm a doer, a goer, not a waiter. But God expects me to "be strong and take heart and wait." So, I decided I would try it. Not only at dryers, but at red lights, in traffic tie-ups, and in the grocery line.

You might try what I began to do: Pray for a person at every "wait" time. A long red light? Pray for that person you blithely promised, "I'll pray for you."

233

After a while, I had a set route to drive home from the office. It had the same red lights every morning and late afternoon. I've gotten very comfortable at "my wife's light" and "the light" for each of my children. In fact, at times, I kind of hope the lights will be red a little longer. I arrive home in a totally different frame of mind.

Red lights belong to my family. Dryers belong to the special needs in our church family. Traffic jams are still an area I'm working on!

John Bunyan said, "If you have not quiet in your mind, outward comfort will do no more for us than a golden slipper on a gouty foot."

Lord Jesus, help me to learn to wait; to acknowledge that you are Lord of circumstances. Teach me to tie together waiting and praying. May my waiting renew my strength to serve you. Amen.

Real Treasures

Wes Haystead

Lay up for yourselves treasures in heaven, where
neither moth nor rust destroys, and where
thieves do not break in or steal; for where
your treasure is, there will your heart be also.
Matthew 6:19-21, *NASB*

We were on vacation in the Santa Cruz Mountains, taking a walk to enjoy the beauties of the redwoods. Our two boys each brought along a paper bag to collect "treasures" they might find along the path. I anticipated they would gather a few bright feathers, some bark of varied textures, some leaves with pungent odors. I was not prepared to see them loading up their bags with big chunks of sandstone.

"We're starting a collection," five-year-old Jonathan announced.

The bags of sandstone made it back to the cabin and into the trunk of the car and were unloaded in our garage at home, treated as objects of great value. (The sandstone finally ended up being delightfully useful in drawing designs on the driveway and sidewalks.)

As I watched the saga of the sandstone, I began to wonder about some of the things I value as I walk through life. Am I collecting things of relatively little value and passing by some far greater treasures?

Have I learned to estimate the worth of things from God's perspective? Are my affections and desires directed toward things of true worth, or do I allow myself to be enchanted by temporary baubles, which will ultimately crumble like chunks of sandstone?

As I live today, Father, help me to see things as you do, so that I may learn to discern and cherish the real treasures. Amen.

Mediating a Broken Window

Michael B. Reynolds

*For there is one God and one mediator
between God and men, the man Christ Jesus.*
1 Timothy 2:5 *NIV*

As soon as I heard the breaking glass, I headed for
the front yard. My six-year-old son, Chad, had thrown the
baseball, and his friend, Johnny, had missed it. The
basement window in the house next door was broken.

Our neighbor, Mr. Freds, was a cranky old man. We
knew where our lot line was because he had pointed it
out to us so often, particularly if Chad's bike or frisbee or
G.I. Joe men were left anywhere close by. Chad knew of
our neighbor's wrath, and when I said we would have to
go over and apologize, Chad begged me not to go.

As I spoke to Mr. Freds through the screen door, Chad
clung to my legs and tried to hide behind me. In the
shadows I could see the ball in the old man's hand and

the angry look on his face. After my apology and offer to pay for the damage, there was complete silence for a moment. Then Mr. Freds let loose with scalding remarks about my failure as a parent and the unruly kids in the neighborhood of which my son was one. As he unleashed his anger, I could hear Chad's quiet sobs in the background.

Finally, Mr. Freds calmed down, and once again I offered my apologies. And then something happened, which I had not expected. Mr. Freds emerged from behind the screen door, handed the ball back to Chad, and told him to be more careful. And as we talked about my picking up the broken glass and buying a new pane, the conversation drifted to when Mr. Freds was a kid and played baseball. Before he was through, I had stood for almost half an hour listening to our neighbor's life history. When it was time to leave, we were laughing and Mr. Freds told me not to hurry on the window.

This experience helped me realize the role Christ plays in our lives as our mediator before God. Certainly God is not like Mr. Freds, but His anger against sin is clear and decisive. Just as I had taken the lead with Chad, Christ leads the way in arranging for God's forgiveness. Christ receives the wrath that is caused by our sins. At first the result is pain, but then comes reconciliation and restoration. We are privileged to enjoy peace with God because of Christ's substitute work on our behalf.

Thank you, Lord, for serving as my mediator and for providing a relationship with you that is filled with peace and joy rather than fear and anger. Amen.

Deacon Reid

Lawrence A. Tucker

And when the Chief Shepherd appears, you will
receive the crown of glory that will never fade.
1 Peter 5:4, *NIV*

He led the congregational singing in the great
church. Smiling, affable Deacon Reid communicated
goodwill and challenge to the worshipers. His ruddy
complexion, with hair whitened by the snow of many
winters, added interest and dignity to his stature.

On this evening we had sung two stanzas of the hymn
"What If It Were Today?" With spirits lifted and
anticipation heightened, we followed his direction into
the opening clause of the third stanza. "Faithful and true
would He find us here..." At that point, to our dismay,
Deacon Reid slowly sank to the platform, a smile playing
on his silent lips. A hush swept the congregation. We who
had been honored and served by a faithful deacon for
more than a generation witnessed his entrance into glory,
still "faithful and true."

It comes to me now how much my life has depended

upon the many others who have been faithful and true. My parents, godly, and devoted to eight children; my wife, a living example of integrity and commitment during our fifty-four years together; a faithful merchant who years ago gave time and talent as a teacher of a class of junior boys; understanding pastors whose love and devotion made real the things of eternity; children who opened new vistas of love, caring, and concern.

There were others also. Who can forget co-workers in the kingdom, partners in prayer, helpers in doing?

How poor my life would have been without the company of the "faithful and true" who have been God's guideposts along the way.

My Father, help me to respond to those whose faithfulness have blessed me by offering that faithfulness and truth to all whom I influence. Amen.

Why?

Robert E. Osman

And Gideon said to him, "Pray, sir, if the Lord is
with us, why then has all this befallen us?"
                    Judges 6:13, *RSV*

Are there times when you feel nothing can go right?
Just when you thought you saw light at the end of the
tunnel, the tunnel caved in?

Why? This is a question I've heard many times as a
minister and Navy chaplain — from homes to hospital
beds, from the battlefields of Vietnam to the cemeteries of
America, from families broken by death or divorce to
young service people, from non-Christians to Christians,
alike. And my answer has to be, I don't know why. Only
God knows why.

I do know that absence of joy does not mean the
absence of God. He's with us every step of the way and
He understands our hurts and feelings. He even
understands when we question. Hebrews 4:15 tells us
"We have a High Priest who is touched with the feeling of
our weaknesses." Yes, God is with us.

The young man Gideon in the Old Testament questioned, too. Gideon worked in the fields beating out grain with a flail. But the Midianites would hunt out anyplace seed had been planted and destroy the crops. On one such occasion, Gideon was dark with sorrow, resentment, and anger. Then a stranger appeared to him and said, "The Lord is with you mighty man of valor."

Gideon responded, "The Lord with me? If so, why has He allowed all this to happen? Why has He forsaken our land? If the Lord is with us, why?"

Maybe Bobby Jones, the basketball great, has the right answer. When awarded by Philadelphia sports writers the Most Courageous Athlete Award of the Year in 1984, Bobby spoke of his epilepsy: "Anything God has created or allowed to happen will be used for good. You can still be successful and lead a fairly active life with this illness. Maybe that's one of the reasons I have it."

Perhaps the answer to the question *why* lies not in what answers we receive but rather in another question. Knowing God is with us in our circumstances, how are we going to deal with our dilemmas?

Lord, I may ask the question, why, this day. But even as I do I know you are with me. I want to learn to accept my present circumstances and keep on pressing on for you. Amen.

A Compass for the Fogs of Life

Dick Hagerman

*No temptation has seized you except what is
common to man. And God is faithful; he will not let
you be tempted beyond what you can bear. But
when you are tempted, he will also provide a way
out so that you can stand up under it.*
1 Corinthians 10:13, *NIV*

My first archery hunt was deep in the heart of
Idaho's Sawtooth Mountains.

I stood beside the saddle of a pine-splotched ridge and
peered through ragged lodgepole pine branches at a
huge Yellowstone elk bull. His massive horns rested
against his back as he stretched out his barreled black
neck. Steam spewed from his mouth as he bugled a four-
octave "Whe-e-e-e-unk" into the misty dawn.

The sight of the majestic animal and the sound of his
high-pitched squeal and cistern-deep grunt accelerated

my heart. The back of my neck prickled like it was entertaining a new hatch of spiders.

I turned and took a compass reading on the white-walled tent we camped in. Now I was ready to hunt.

After two hours of stalking through the crowded lodgepole pines, a heavy fog shut off my vision. There was no hope of finding the elk, and my compass was the only hope of finding camp. Would I trust it? Could I believe it pointed true?

I had no choice but to trust and believe its readings, and when I did, it led me back to camp.

As I've stalked through some fogs of life — rebuilding a burned-out office, grieving over a daughter's sudden death, worrying about a post-retirement syndrome — I've found in God's Word a compass I can trust and believe. It has led me back to God's camp when life seemed hopeless.

Heavenly Father, grant me the wisdom to trust and believe that your word will lead me through life's fogs to your camp. Amen.

Home, Where We Belong

Brad Sargent

*God Himself will be with them and shall wipe away
every tear from their eyes. Death shall be no longer,
nor mourning, nor crying, nor any further pain,
because the former things have passed away.*
Revelation 21:3-4, *MLB*

I knew little more about Dave than two crucial facts:
his wife of several years drowned in a river-rafting
accident ten weeks earlier and Dave committed his life to
Christ that same day.

I dialed nervously. The phone at the other end started
ringing. "I can't believe I'm doing this, Lord! If he's not
there by six rings, I'm hanging up."

"Hello."

"Hi. Is this Dave?"

"Yeah."

"Well, Dave, you don't know me, but my name's Brad...."

Now, I'm as fidgety about dealing with death as the next person, but somehow I knew God wanted me to reach out to Dave. So I phoned and invited him over for coffee. Not until his third visit did Dave share the traumatic details of Nan's drowning. Numbed, all I could do was listen, something Dave later told me few others had been willing to do.

God continued to tie our lives together through many conversations, shared meals, hymn sings, garnet digs, helping each other pack and move. All this time I watched and listened and prayed for Dave's healing.

Gradually, God replaced grief with wholeness. Two years after Nan's death, Dave stopped wearing his wedding band. Two more years and he finally showed me photographs of her. Nearly two years later, Dave was dating Kerri, a wonderful woman from his home fellowship group. Dave phoned me a few months later — asking if I would be best man at their wedding!

On December 31 we stood side by side in our tuxedos. Because of our history as friends, the entire ceremony triggered deep emotions for me. Holding back the tears proved difficult. Finally, the wedding party recessed down the aisle. I looked Dave in the eyes, smiled despite the lump in my throat, and hugged him while our tears flowed freely. That hug was my way of telling him, "You've been restored, Dave! Welcome home, buddy!"

Jesus watches and listens and prays for us as we go through various sufferings. What a comfort — we can tell the Great Physician all the things no one else cares to hear and He dispenses the healing balm we need. And I envisioned when the time comes to pass into His presence, He will reach out, clasp each one of us close to

Himself, and gently whisper, "My child, you've passed the test! Welcome home!"

Thank you, Lord Jesus, you remain with me through my trials on earth and are there in person to welcome me home to heaven. Help me to remember that suffering is temporary, but joy is eternal. Amen.

Between Blessings

Tony Sbrana

*This is a trustworthy saying that deserves full
acceptance (and for this we labor and strive), that
we have put our hope in the living God, who is the
Savior of all men, and especially of those who
believe.* 1 Timothy 4:9-10, *NIV*

"So, what do you do?"

An innocent and common enough question. But if
you're unemployed, it can be a little awkward saying,
"Well, actually, I'm out of work right now." That kind of
admission cuts to the quick of the male ego.

The reply I prefer is, "I'm between jobs." I like that. It's
optimistic. And it implies that you're taking steps to
remedy the situation. When I was single and home alone
on a Saturday night, I'd tell people I was "between dates."
Same idea.

And I wonder if we wouldn't do well to have that kind
of attitude in our spiritual lives. For instance, has God
been silent for a time? Fine. You're "between answers."
Has it been awhile since you've experienced the power of

God in or around your life? Fine. You're "between miracles." I'm not suggesting that you just sit back on your laurels and spout platitudes. As I said before, this attitude implies that you're taking steps towards a solution. You're continuing to pray. You're continuing to listen. You're continuing to obey. But mostly, you're continuing to believe...to *believe* in the unflagging faithfulness of God.

You remain optimistic. Well, actually, optimistic isn't the right word. It smacks too much of secular humanism. And, besides, too many people are optimistic by nature, hoping that things will work out for good even when there's absolutely no reason. Believers aren't optimistic. They're "theoptimistic." They have a reason to hope. God! And it is God who has promised that, for those who love and follow Him, He will work things out for good (Romans 8:28).

Are you between answers? Are you between miracles? Hang in there. Be "theoptimistic"! God's mercies are new every morning.

Father, I confess my tendency to grow impatient in times of dryness or silence. Forgive me, and help me to realize anew just who I have placed my hope in: the living God who will never leave or forsake me. Amen.

MEET OUR CONTRIBUTORS

Don M. Aycock is an avid fisherman who loves the outdoors, traveling, and writing. He is the author of several books including *Walking Straight in a Crooked World, Apathy in the Pews,* and *Heralds to a New Age.* Don and his wife, Carla, have twin boys and make their home in Lake Charles, Louisiana.

Bob Baker is an "omnivorous" reader, a "dedicated" trout fisherman and enjoys family hiking and backpacking. He has written several magazine articles and stories. Bob is a pastor and teaches Bible at Maranatha High School in Sierra Madre. He and his wife, Marlene, have five children and reside in Covina, California.

Robert Beckwith is a student at Golden Gate University in San Francisco where he's enrolled in their aviation and operations management program. He is a certified flight instructor and, in his free time, enjoys water skiing, snow skiing, and boating. He makes his home in Ventura, California.

Ray Beeson is president and director of Overcomers Ministries and travels extensively, teaching primarily on prayer and spiritual warfare. He is the author of the books *The Real Battle* and *That I May Know Him.* Ray enjoys hunting and fishing. He and his wife, Linda, make their home in Ventura, California. They have four children.

James E. Bolton, besides writing, enjoys theological studies, bicycling, racquetball, volleyball, and gardening. In addition, he has a nursing home ministry. James is a member of the Evangelical Theological Society and the Washington Christian Writers Fellowship. He lives in Spokane, Washington.

Charles R. Brown writes a weekly article for his church and has written action spots for local radio. He enjoys art and music, both as a listener and programmer. Charles works for a title insurance company, is an elder in his church, and teaches Sunday School. He and his wife, Bobbie, have four children and live in Riverside, California.

Tom Carter, besides being the compiler and editor of *Spurgeon at His Best,* is the author of four other books, including *For Members Only: A Guide to Responsible Church Membership,* and more than 50 articles. Tom is a pastor, husband, and father. He and his wife, Mary, have two daughters and make their home in Dinuba, California.

Larry E. Clark directs the Christian Writers Fellowship of Orange County (California)

251

and is a 32-year veteran missionary with Wycliffe Bible Translators. He is the author of the book *Not Silenced by Darkness* and numerous articles and short stories. Larry and his wife, Nancy, have three children and reside in Santa Ana, California.

Richard Cornelius is a retired school teacher who enjoys reading, walking, traveling, and spending time with his five children and nine grandchildren. He and his wife, Ethel, have been married 42 years. They make their home in Simi Valley, California.

Leonard W. DeWitt has written numerous articles and enjoys reading, sports, and being with his family. He is a pastor who says, "I love to laugh and cry with people and help them solve their problems." Leonard and his wife, Joyce, reside in Ventura, California. They have two grown children and one grandson.

James C. Dobson is founder and president of Focus on the Family and can be heard daily on his radio program, by the same name, on more than 1000 stations. He has written several books, including *Hide or Seek, The Strong Willed Child, Straight Talk to Men and Their Wives,* and *Love Must Be Tough.* Dr. Dobson and his wife, Shirley, make their home in Southern California. The Dobsons have two grown children.

Dan Driver has had several articles published. Besides writing he enjoys public speaking, bowling, swimming, and reading—"especially history and biographies." Dan is a directory assistance operator with U.S. West Communications and makes his home in Mesa, Arizona.

Donald L. Evans, Jr., works in sales and has had two articles published. He enjoys music, cooking, sports, camping, and fishing. In addition, he sings in a men's quartet at Glenkirk Presbyterian Church in Glendora, California. Donald makes his home in nearby San Dimas.

Dave Grant is an author and has been involved in human resource development for over twenty-five years. He presents over one hundred in-house seminars yearly to executive, management, and sales personnel and makes several more appearances as a featured speaker. Dave resides in California with his wife, Simone, and their four children.

Dick Hagerman has had numerous magazine and newspaper articles published. A dentist of 37 years, Dick has also been a lay preacher and elder in the United Presbyterian Church. He enjoys writing, bow hunting, fishing, and square dancing. He and his wife, Dorothy, have two daughters and four granddaughters. The Hagermans reside in Wendell, Idaho.

Edward L. Hayes is the executive director of Mount Hermon Association, a Christian camp and conference center. He has written two books and numerous articles. He enjoys horticulture, art, ornithology, botany, photography, and music. Edward and his wife, Marilyn, who reside at Mount Hermon, California, have three grown children.

Wes Haystead has written several articles and books including *Teaching Your Child About God* and *The Church Computer Manual.* He enjoys reading, walking, cooking, and sports. Wes is editorial director for a firm serving the computer needs of churches. He and his wife, Sheryl, have one daughter and two sons and reside in Ventura, California.

David H. Hepburn hosts a weekly radio program in San Francisco. Currently the president of Bridgemont High School and Foundation, he has been in education, the ministry, and missions for 35 years. In addition, he is a member of the Covenant Four Quartet. David and his wife, Daisy, have two grown children and make their home in San Francisco.

Glenn W. Hoerr is an associate pastor for Twin Lakes Baptist Church in Aptos, California, where he's involved in singles/adult education. In addition, he writes and edits his church's monthly newsletter. He enjoys playing and watching sports, gardening, reading, and playing table games. He and his wife, Jeanne, have three children and make their home in Capitola, California.

Stephen H. Holbrook is president of Princeton Management Associates and is a consultant to over two hundred banks and corporations. In addition to being a speaker, he has written four books and numerous articles. Stephen is active in local government and enjoys restoring antique cars and playing tennis. He and his wife, Elaine, have three grown daughters and reside in the Princeton, New Jersey area.

Jonathan Kattenhorn edits a quarterly newsletter and has many articles concerning the handicapped published in magazines and take-home papers. Besides writing, Jonathan enjoys camping, woodworking, and farming. He has completed a two-year home Bible course through Liberty Home Bible Institute. Jonathan makes his home in Shafter, California.

Josh McDowell is the author of twenty-eight books, including *Evidence that Demands a Verdict, More than a Carpenter,* and *Evidence for Joy.* He has appeared before over seven million young people in seventy-four countries. Besides representing Campus Crusade for Christ, he heads Josh McDowell Ministries. The McDowells have four children and reside in California.

Mark McLean is a musician who tours with Wings of Morning, a division of the Family Outreach Ministries of Ventura, California. Mark enjoys all sports and "working with people." As a member of Wings of Morning, Mark has ministered to people all across the United States and abroad. He makes his home in Ventura.

Al Munger, recently retired, was a pastor for thirty-two years. He has written for *Viewpoint* magazine and enjoys RV travel, woodworking, and computers. He and his wife, Erika, make their home in Poulsbo, Washington. They have two married daughters and four grandsons.

Lloyd John Ogilvie is senior pastor of the First Presbyterian Church of Hollywood, California. He can be seen on his weekly television program, "Let God Love You," and is the author of several books, including *You Are Loved and Forgiven, You Can Pray With Power,* and *A Future and a Hope.* Dr. Ogilvie and his wife, Mary Jane, reside in Hollywood. They have three children.

Ray Ortlund is president of Renewal Ministries in Newport Beach, California and president/speaker of the *Haven of Rest* radio broadcast. He is the author of many books including *Lord, Make My Life a Miracle* and *Be a New Christian*

All Your Life. A pastor for many years, he ministers the world over. He and his wife, Anne, are the parents of four grown childern and reside in Corona del Mar, California.

Robert E. Osman is a retired U.S. Navy captain—and chaplain—and serves as an interim pastor for the Presbyterian Church. He enjoys woodworking, golf, and reading, and, with his wife, Esther, has conducted seminars in marriage enrichment. The Osmans have three children and six grandchildren. They reside in Ventura, California.

Michael B. Reynolds is the editor for *Emphasis on Faith and Living*, the official publication of the Missionary Church. He enjoys fishing, reading, and science. Previously, he has served as a pastor, associate college professor, and director of Christian education. He and his wife, Sherri, have one son and make their home in Markle, Indiana.

Herman D. Rosenberger has spent 30 years in pastoral ministry. He is an author of adult curriculum and has written numerous articles for the Foursquare *World Advance* magazine. He enjoys photography, bicycling, and jogging and is an avid reader. He is a husband, father of four and grandfather of eight. He and his wife, Margaret, reside in Ventura, California.

W. James Russell has written technical and marketing articles for trade publications. He is a pilot and the president of Amy Foundation. Jim has a deep interest in challenging Christian writers to carry God's truth to the world through secular communications media. He and his wife, Phyllis, have five children. They make their home in Lansing, Michigan.

Harold J. Sala is founder and president of Guidelines, Inc., an international Christian ministry reaching into at least 80 countries of the world through radio, television, seminars, and books. He enjoys tennis, golf, biking, and walking. Harold and his wife, Darlene, have three grown children and make their home in Mission Viejo, California.

Brad Sargent has a variety of interests besides writing, which include music, operatic whistling, cooking, puns, and "making people laugh." He has written and performed a one-act musical comedy for the Wycliffe Summer Institute in Linguistics at Dallas. Brad resides in Spokane, Washington.

Tony Sbrana is on the staff of Young Life in the San Francisco Bay Area, working with high school and college students in Oakland and Berkeley. He enjoys playing the guitar and keyboard, and writes and performs Christian and popular music. He and his wife, Michelle, make their home in Lafayette, California.

James L. Snyder, a former pastor, has published articles in numerous magazines and is currently writing a biography of A. W. Tozer. James enjoys reading, speaking, and writing. He and his wife, Martha, have two daughters and one son. The Snyders make their home in Glen Burnie, Maryland.

John R. Strubhar is senior pastor of Calvary Church of Pacific Palisades, California. He has written numerous magazine articles and co-authored the book *Evangelistic Preaching: A Step by Step Guide to Pulpit Evangelism*. He enjoys golf, tennis, and reading. John and his wife, Sandra, have three daughters and reside in Pacific Palisades.

Charles R. Swindoll is a widely-known author, pastor, and radio minister. He is senior pastor of the First Evangelical Free Church in Fullerton, California, and can be heard daily on Insight for Living. He is the author of several books, including *Improving Your Serve, Growing Strong in the Seasons of Life,* and *Living Above the Level of Mediocrity.* The Swindolls reside in Southern California.

Leif A. Tangvald is a student at Eastern Washington University, where he is majoring in business. Leif is active in Young Life and enjoys music, singing, sports, and playing the guitar. He and his family make their home in Spokane, Washington.

Lawrence A. Tucker is a former Baptist pastor and has contributed many articles to the *Baptist Message.* He enjoys public speaking, teaching the Scriptures, writing, and such sports as golf, volleyball, and tennis. He and Nancy, his wife of fifty-four years, have two daughters and one son. The Tuckers make their home in Memphis, Tennessee.

W. Terry Whalin is the associate editor for *In Other Words,* the flagship publication of Wycliffe Bible Translators. He has written numerous magazine articles and is a book reviewer. Terry is an amateur radio operator and enjoys reading, collecting pocket knives, and running. He and his wife, Gaylyn, have two sons. They reside in Costa Mesa, California.

Grayson F. Wyly is retired from the 3M Company, where he worked with patents. Besides writing, he enjoys swimming, boating, fishing, and gardening. He and his wife, Louise, have two daughters and two sons and four grandchildren. The Wylys reside in Minneapolis, Minnesota.

POSTSCRIPT

I Met My Master Face to Face

I had walked life's path with an easy tread,
*   Had followed where comfort and pleasure led;*
And then by chance in a quiet place—
*   I met my Master face to face.*

With station and rank and wealth for goal,
*   Much thought for body but none for soul,*
I had entered to win this life's mad race—
*   When I met my Master face to face.*

I had built my castles, reared them high,
*   Till their towers had pierced the blue of the sky;*
I had sworn to rule with an iron mace—
*   When I met my Master face to face.*

I met Him and knew Him, and blushed to see
*   That His eyes full of sorrow were fixed on me;*
And I faltered, and fell at His feet that day
*   While my castles vanished and melted away.*

Melted and vanished; and in their place
*   I saw naught else but my Master's face;*
And I cried aloud: "Oh, make me meet
*   To follow the marks of Thy wounded feet."*

My thought is now for the souls of men;
*   I have lost my life to find it again*
Ever since alone in that holy place
*   My Master and I stood face to face.*

— Author Unknown

It's our prayer that, as you've read through the pages of this book, you've come to know the Master a little better.

Clint and Mary Beckwith